HOMEMADE
BUSINESS

FOCUS ON THE FAMILY®

renewing
the heart™

HOMEMADE BUSINESS

DONNA PARTOW

TYNDALE
Tyndale House Publishers, Wheaton, Illinois

Homemade Business
Copyright © 1992, 1999 by Donna Partow

Partow, Donna
    Homemade business : a woman's step-by-step
guide to earning money at home / Donna Partow
        p. cm.
    Includes bibliographical references.
    ISBN 1-56179-713-8
    1. Home-based businesses—United States. 2.
Women-owned business enterprises—United States. 3.
New business enterprises—United States. 4. Work and
family—United States. I. Title.
    HD2336.U5P37 1992
    658'.041—dc20

A Focus on the Family book published by Tyndale House
Publishers, Wheaton, Illinois.

Printed in the United States of America
99 00 01 02 03/10 9 8 7 6 5 4 3 2

This book is lovingly dedicated to the two most important people in my life:

*my husband, Cameron,
and my daughter, Leah.*

Other Books by Donna Partow

A Woman's Guide to the Temperaments
Becoming a Vessel God Can Use
Families that Play Together Stay Together
*How to Work with the One You Love and Live to
    Tell About It*
No More Lone Ranger Moms
Walking in Total God-Confidence

Contents

Acknowledgments ix
Introduction xi
Introduction to the Second Edition xiii

PART I: SO YOU WANT TO WORK AT HOME
  1. The High Cost of Being a Working Mother. . 3
  2. The Advantages of Homework 11
  3. Managing Your Time 21
  4. Your Children and Your Business. 43
  5. Keys to Success 57

PART II: ESSENTIAL DETAILS OF A HOME-BASED BUSINESS
  6. Laying a Solid Business Foundation. . . . 75
  7. Marketing. 89
  8. Your Home Office 121
  9. Do You Need a Computer?. 139
 10. The Wonderful World Online 149
 11. Legal Issues 157
 12. Finances 165

PART III: CONSIDERING THE OPTIONS
 13. FAQs: Frequently Asked Questions About
      Working from Home 189

14. Information Technologies 199
15. Service Industries 205
16. Direct Sales 211
17. Business Support Services 219
18. A New Era for Women Entrepreneurs . 227

Part IV: Launching Your Business

19. Hundreds of Things You Can
    Do from Home 237
20. Business and Home Management
    Forms 247
21. Resources Available to You 267
22. Recommended Reading List 273
    Notes 275

Acknowledgments

Special thanks: To my parents, Jack and Olga Power, for believing in my dreams. Who knows? Maybe this book will hit the best-seller list and we'll buy that boat after all!

To my sister, Helen—confidante, cheerleader, and birthing coach extraordinaire! Thanks for lending a hand when I needed it most.

To my family in Christ, the Rileys, for love and support far above the call of duty. With extra special thanks to:

Beth, the world's greatest proofreader. Amy, for keeping my house clean in spite of me. Linda, for taking such good care of Leah.

To all the women who have allowed their stories to be told on the pages of this book.

To the wonderful team at Focus on the Family, in order of appearance: Larry Weeden, for giving me a chance; Janet Kobobel, for lending her enthusiasm and market savvy to the project; and Keith Wall, for making me look like a better writer than I am.

To my heavenly Father, who has so graciously granted me the desires of my heart.

"Ah, Sovereign Lord, you have made the heavens and the earth by your great power and outstretched arm. Nothing is too hard for you."

—*Jeremiah 32:17*

Acknowledgments

Introduction

One of the most common questions people asked me during my first pregnancy was, "Are you going to work after the baby arrives?" People were intrigued when I responded that, yes, I was going to work, but I planned to do so from my home. Almost without exception, the women I talked with expressed a strong interest in combining career and family by working at home. Yet they didn't know how to go about making that dream a reality.

I undertook to write this book because I am convinced working at home is a viable option for many women today. As America moves beyond a factory- and office-based economy into the information age, the economic center of society is returning to the home (as it was during the agriculture-based colonial period). The explosive growth of the Internet makes working at home an increasingly realistic possibility for millions of Americans. In fact, it is estimated that some 50 million Americans already work at home, and the numbers grow larger each day.

At this juncture, the only obstacle to home work is innovation and novelty. People are always resistant to change, even when it's actually a return to a previous way of life. But change must come, and fortunate are those who sense the wave coming in time to ride it.

Will you be one of those who seize the moment?

Introduction to the Second Edition

When I initially wrote *Homemade Business* back in 1990, the idea of working from home was novel, perhaps even suspect. "I work from home" was just another way of saying "I can't find a real job." Dot-matrix printers were the order of the day, fax machines spit out curled thermal paper, and the Internet was still considered science fiction.

What a difference a decade makes. As we move into the new millennium, working from home is in vogue. My humble home business was once the brunt of family jokes. (I can only imagine what the *neighbors* and my *former coworkers* were saying!) Today, I'm making four times as much money as I did when I worked for corporate America and leading a lifestyle most Americans only dream about. And I'm not just talking about money, although my home business became our primary income during the early 1990s, when my husband endured several long years of unemployment and underemployment. Working from home is, for our family, central to our way of life.

My first home office was a 3x5-foot closet in a tiny one-bedroom apartment. No kidding! From there, I graduated to a separate bedroom in our three-bedroom trailer. Today, I'm sitting in my 24x24-foot office, located in a separate building across from my cedar cabin in the mountains.

From the time I was a little girl, I dreamed of being a writer, living in a cabin on the side of a mountain. Through the blessing of my home business, God has been gracious to transform that dream into a reality.

We live on two acres of land in Northern Arizona, where we home-school our three children amidst the largest stand of ponderosa pines in the world. The air is so fresh that we can taste it, and we enjoy sunshine and blue skies year round. The view out my office windows is so spectacular that I can hardly believe this is *my* life. No more inner city, no more overcrowded suburbs; we can live wherever we choose. Of course, if you *want* to live in the city or the suburbs, wonderful! But isn't it nice to know you have a choice?

Recently, while driving home after a visit with friends, my husband and I began talking about our oldest daughter, Nichole, now 16. We took her into our home five years ago, when she was left homeless because both of her parents went to prison.

"It's amazing what a combination of both of us she has become," my husband remarked. "She has your passion for God, for ministry. . . ." I finished his sentence: "And she has your ability to deal with people." We, as her parents, are the greatest influence in her life. She is becoming like us because she spends most of her time with us.

We are noticing the same pattern with our younger children. Leah, 9, shares my passion for justice and my husband's love for music. Three-year-old Taraneh is as bossy as her mom and as charming as her dad! If I was off working in an office, my children wouldn't become like me—they'd become like their peers. Working from home means our children know us and share our values.

I love the fact that my life isn't fragmented like the lives of so many women I meet. I have one world, and my family is part of it. I love the fact that my children know exactly where the money comes from—and how hard it is to come by. I think they value their possessions much more because they see, daily, what it takes to provide them.

Last year, Nichole launched her own home business making cloth bookmarks to raise $5,000 for a mission trip to Africa. Our whole family got involved in the "manufacturing" process. She sold nearly 4,000 bookmarks and now has a profound appreciation of what it really takes to get to the mission field.

When I receive letters from readers—especially from prisoners or other people enduring hard times—my daughter Leah loves to draw pictures to send them. She recently created beautiful stained-glass angels to send to a group of female prisoners who are studying my book *Becoming a Vessel God Can Use*. Leah feels she's a vital part of my work and ministry—and she is.

Such moments are, for me, the most significant blessing of my homemade business . . .

because my greatest homemade business is the business of raising children.

If the lifestyle I'm describing appeals to you, you've picked up the right book. The first edition of *Homemade Business* helped tens of thousands of women launch their own home businesses. If you're ready to leave the workplace, or you're already a stay-at-home mom who doesn't want to return to the workplace, you hold a helpful, proven resource in your hands.

I have to warn you, though: It won't happen overnight. There's no one to "hire you," and no one will hand you a home business. You'll have to work long, hard hours; maybe harder than you've ever worked in your life. However, you can successfully launch your own business if you're willing to work through—not just *read* through, but *work* through—the steps outlined on the following pages.

It's my prayer that today will be the beginning of a whole new adventure and a whole new way of life for you and your family. Godspeed on your journey!

Part One

So You Want to Work at Home

CHAPTER ONE

The High Cost of Being a Working Mother

In recent years, a growing number of women have felt torn between the conflicting demands of career and family. Today, financial and societal pressures require the majority of women to return to work before their baby is one year old. Women who opt to stay home often do so at great financial sacrifice. Unfortunately, the tendency has been to present this as an either-or proposition: Either you pursue a career outside of your home or you forgo any opportunity to earn money (and other career benefits) to stay home with your children. However, there is another option. You can combine career and family by working at home.

Every day, I hear from mothers who say, "I so much want to be home with my kids, but I just can't afford it. We need my income." No doubt that's true in some cases. When my husband was unemployed, and then seriously *under*employed for several years, I became the primary bread-winner in our family. However, many women who think they "have to work" simply haven't done the math. Larry Burkett, author of *Women Leaving the Workplace,* did extensive research on this issue. Following are his statistics on the high cost of being a working mother:

Expense	Monthly Amount
Child care	$450[1]
Transportation	$250
Work-related clothing	$50
Additional eating out	$80
Misc. (lunches, office gifts, etc.)	$60
Household help	$25
	$915 per month

Okay, now for the really frightening part: The median income for working moms is only $14,500. Bottom line? Most working women bring home an extra $300 per month, if they're lucky. Based on a 40-hour work week, that comes out to $2 per hour. I vaguely remember the corporate grind (it's been 10 years since this woman left the workplace), but I'm certain of one thing: You'd have to pay *me* at least $200 per hour to put up with all the hassles, headaches, and heartaches involved. In my opinion, it just isn't worth it.

Well, you might be thinking, *some working moms make a lot more than that! I'll bet it's well worth it for them.* Not so. Burkett cites a report in the *Chicago Tribune:* "Even in families where the primary wage earner makes $100,000 and the secondary wage earner makes $50,000, nearly 80 percent of the second income is consumed in taxes, child care, and transportation."

I hope these numbers shock you into reality. Ladies, we are giving up the greatest responsibility and highest privilege in the world—raising our own children. And for what? The joy of being perpetually exhausted and the thrill of ordering out for pizza.

Moms, let's wake up and read the bottom line. And for those of you who are yearning to be at home but your husband doesn't think you can afford it, I urge you to show him these statistics. Then he'll know the truth about the bottom line.

When you work from home, even if your income is significantly lower than that of your former job, you can still come out ahead in the financial game, because you will dramatically reduce your expenses.

The Impossible Dream?

Many women view working at home as an impossible dream. They conjure up a thousand reasons why it won't work for them: They lack self-discipline, they're not smart enough, they don't know how to get started. It's a lot easier, and much less frightening, to get a safe and secure nine-to-five job. True, there are risks in starting a new home business, however small or large. But with those risks come opportunities to be your own boss, set your schedule, launch a new career, and be accessible to your children.

People no longer see a home-based business as a last resort or meager sideline. In fact, it has become a very enviable alternative.

One Who Dared

Marcia Cone-Esaki is the perfect example of a woman whose perseverance has paid off in a big way. After seven years of working full time, Marcia decided she'd had enough of corporate America. So she turned her love of writing and cooking (along with training in foods and nutrition) into a home-based business. But success didn't come overnight for her and her partner, Thelma Snyder. They struggled for five years, during which time Marcia lived with relatives and often exchanged baby-sitting and household chores for rent.

Things changed dramatically for Marcia when she landed a publishing deal for her third cookbook with a major publisher, Simon & Schuster. To date, *Mastering Microwave Cookery* has sold over 100,000 copies. Altogether, her five cookbooks have sold more than a quarter of a million copies. She has appeared on the "Today" show three times and has been appointed a national

spokesperson for The Potato Board and the
Campbell Soup Company.

Marcia's articles and recipes have appeared in
Redbook, Ladies' Home Journal, House Beautiful
and *Working Mother,* just to mention a few. Her
work has been praised in publications nationwide,
including *People* magazine, *Food & Wine, The
Chicago Tribune* and *The Baltimore Sun Times.
The Philadelphia Inquirer* heralded *Mastering
Microwave Cookery* as the preeminent cookbook
for the microwave generation.

Her professional success has enriched her personal life as well. For example, Marcia's husband,
Koji, enrolled full time in seminary to study for the
pastorate. Marcia's income from royalties, speaking fees, and an advance on a forthcoming book
will largely support their entire family of four.

"I can't imagine a better arrangement than what
I have," Marcia says. "I am home with my family,
but I occasionally get away to travel on business. I
use a minimum of child care, and I can move anywhere with my work, depending on my husband's
needs. I know this work is a gift from the Lord,
and more than once when I thought about giving it
up, He has encouraged me to keep going."

Making It Happen

By purchasing this book, you have already
taken the first step to establishing your own home
business. In the following chapters, you will learn
everything you need to know to plan and launch a

home business: how to choose a business that is right for you, developing a business plan, time management tips, marketing, cutting through legal red tape, laying a solid financial foundation, and much more. You'll also find reproducible forms and charts to help you organize your business and household.

At the end of each chapter, you will find questions to help you clarify pertinent issues and discern the direction of your business. Some chapters also include assignments, enabling you to lay a business foundation in bite-size chunks. I highly recommend that you answer the questions and complete the forms as thoroughly as possible. The more work you do up front, the more likely your business will succeed.

So choose one of the items included on the list of "Hundreds of Things You Can Do from Home" (chapter 19) or invent an idea of your own, and start today to build a better future for yourself and your family.

Questions

1. Why do you want to start a home-based business?

2. What has prevented you from getting started?

3. What do you expect will be the most difficult part?

4. Do you have any possible business ideas right now? If so, list them.

CHAPTER TWO

The Advantages of Homework

Like any job, working at home offers both advantages and disadvantages. In the days and months ahead, times of discouragement will come. Many women struggle with conflicting priorities and time management. And the physical and emotional demands of promoting your business can be draining. You may begin to wonder if all your hard work is worthwhile, and you may even be tempted to give up your plans. In those moments, turn back to this chapter, re-examine the many benefits of working at home, and redouble your efforts to succeed. Remember, anything worth having is worth fighting for.

Be Available for Your Children

The Mothers' Home Business Network conducted a survey of home-based businesswomen, and 98 percent of the respondents agreed that homework is the perfect way to juggle the conflicting demands of work and family. Furthermore, 72 percent indicated that being available for their children is the number-one reason they choose to work at home.

According to Donata Glassmeyer, who leads "Mother's Work at Home" workshops, most of the women she meets are interested in homework because day care is undesirable or inadequate, especially for women with more than one child. She explains: "The second child comes along and day care simply becomes too stressful. First one child is sick, and then the other. The cost is too high; caregivers too unreliable."

By working at home, you can avoid the hassles and costs of day care and enjoy spending time with your children. Even if you have to hire a babysitter to watch your kids in your home while you work, you will be available at a moment's notice if needed. And you can keep a watchful eye on all that goes on throughout the day, rather than sitting at a desk wondering if your children are okay.

Supplement Your Family's Income

According to the U. S. Bureau of Labor Statistics, most American families in 1990 required a second income to make ends meet. Inflation, health insurance, housing, and higher taxes all take a heavy toll on the family income. For some, a home business is ideal, providing flexibility and the opportunity to supplement the family income.

Catherine Smith, proprietor of Cateswear (hand-crafted clothing) and single parent of two, has experienced the benefits of earning money and being available for her children. "To help our family budget, I had been working two jobs, and it was taking its toll on my kids. Now that I work at home, there's a world of difference in their attitudes, motivation, and behavior. They're much more secure just knowing I'm home." Even though it's difficult not having a predictable income, Cate feels the tradeoff is worth it. "When children have only one parent, it's even more important to be available and involved," she says.

Be Your Own Boss

Several years ago, *The Wall Street Journal* ran a cover story on "defensive entrepreneurs"— people who, driven by job insecurity, are starting businesses on the side. These people fear dependence on a corporation because they have seen the rug pulled out from under so many of their colleagues. The days when you could rely on a company to look out for your best interests are long gone. While you're working your fingers to the bone for XYZ Corporation, it is entirely possible they are filling out your pink slip.

I experienced this firsthand when I worked in the investment banking department of a large financial institution. Because the corporation had lost nearly half a billion dollars, some three thousand employees had to be laid off. I knew people who had devoted their entire careers—25 or 30 years of their lives—to this corporation. But when the chips were down, they were out on the street, sometimes without even a day's notice.

Eventually, paranoia virtually paralyzed many of my colleagues, and we spent most of the workday worrying about who would be the next to lose his or her job. At times like that, the emotional burden of relying on someone else to sign my paycheck was heavy indeed.

Once you establish your own home-based business, you'll have the pleasure of signing your own paycheck. And when you think you deserve a raise, you can give yourself one.

Set Your Own Hours

Another advantage of being your own boss is setting your own hours. If you want to sleep late, go ahead (as long as you don't do it too often). Want to take four weeks of vacation this year? No "Policies and Procedures Manual" will spoil your plans. Do you need to quit early on Wednesdays so your daughter can take ballet lessons? No one will stand in your way.

Jean Haven Amos began her career in real estate almost 15 years ago. In the beginning, she worked long hours six days a week and, like most new agents, had to take all the in-office floor time she could get, handling phones and helping walk-in clients. Today, she says, "I don't work any floor time. I'm established enough that I don't need it." As a result, Jean only reports to the office when it's absolutely necessary, such as for weekly staff meetings.

Jean feels that real estate offers her tremendous flexibility, and she finds that a substantial amount of her work can be done from home. "A lot of my business involves phone work," she says. "So I can put a load of wash in and then make calls at my kitchen table." Jean has also set up a desk in her bedroom, where she keeps her paperwork. She finds working at home more efficient than the office, because there are fewer interruptions.

Opportunities for Success

When you work nine to five for someone else's company, to a large extent he or she controls how well you do. But when you work for yourself, only your ability and determination set the limits. Maybe there's something you have always dreamed of doing. Now is your chance to do it. You may aspire only to make a little extra money, but there's always the chance that your "silly idea" will catch on and you'll find yourself transformed into a very successful entrepreneur. Someone has to think up those great ideas. Why not you? Maybe you're planning to launch a new full-time career. What an opportunity to start anew!

I was eventually laid off from my job as an investment-banking representative, and it was one of the best things that ever happened to me. It forced me to look at my life and make decisions about what I really wanted to do. As a result, I went back to college to pursue a writing career. If I hadn't lost that job, I wouldn't be where I am today—and you wouldn't be reading this book.

Mental Stimulation

Let's be honest. No matter how much you love being a mother, changing diapers is not exactly on par with performing brain surgery. It's important to develop interests apart from the daily routine or you may find yourself bored and bitter. If you consider "Gilligan's Island" stimulating or find yourself shouting out letters during "Wheel of Fortune," you are very much in need of constructive nonmaternal activities. What could be more stimulating and rewarding than running your own business?

Anne Hulley, mother of five and creator of Field Trips Greeting Cards, has found that calligraphing her cards not only provides an outlet for artistic expression, but it also stimulates personal growth. "I try to let the Holy Spirit lead as I design each of my cards," she explains. "The Scriptures I choose are a reflection of my own spiritual growth. This way I can combine my business, creativity, and personal growth."

Anne also appreciates the immediacy of her craft: "Parenting is a matter of faith. You pour yourself into your children and hope your efforts will be rewarded someday. This [the greeting card business] is something from which I can quickly see the fruit of my labor."

Continue Your Career

Many women spend years training for a career before their children arrive on the scene. Teachers, nurses, doctors, lawyers, and many other professionals can quite easily transfer their hard-earned skills to a home-based business. Knowing your career is not on hold will give you satisfaction, even though the majority of your time may be spent with family. This is especially important if you want to resume your before-children career.

A Sense of Accomplishment

Believe it or not, God gave the mandate to work before the Fall of Mankind (Gen. 2:15). Productive work is not a punishment but an important part of His plan for our lives. Everyone has experienced that exhilarating feeling of working hard to complete a project or the joy of beholding something you've made with your own hands.. A home business will provide abundant opportunities for you to enjoy that exhilaration.

In the words of Ellen Lane, a home-schooling mother of three who runs a growing franchise of sewing schools, "I have a real sense of accomplishment knowing I have inspired and motivated others to learn a skill they can benefit from for

the rest of their lives." In fact, Ellen is now working with Detroit social workers to teach unwed
mothers how to sew. She hopes many of these
young women will someday start their own
sewing schools—and experience the joy of
accomplishment.

Opportunities for Ministry

A number of women start businesses because
they see a need and believe they can meet it. That
may mean providing services to strengthen individuals or families, or the business itself may be
the ministry.

Patricia LeBlanc, founder of Hazen Road
QuiltWorks, was motivated by a desire to minister
to others. She noticed many of the women at her
Mennonite church in rural Vermont made beautiful handcrafted items. She also noticed that they
were unable to market them profitably and effectively. So she decided to put her marketing skills
to work promoting their quilts, wall hangings, and
other crafts through a direct mail business. That's
how Hazen Road QuiltWorks was born.

Expand Your Sphere of Influence

The most effective way of influencing people
for the gospel is by interacting naturally, in the
course of our daily lives. As your home-based
business gets under way, you will have many
opportunities to demonstrate a Christian lifestyle
to an ever-widening circle of business associates.

One woman who has influenced many is Alberta Benster, founder of Accessories by Alberta. Over the past eight years, Alberta has provided jobs for 15 of her neighbors—all working out of their own homes—through her line of children's accessories.

"One of my primary goals in starting this business was to help widows and women with preschoolers," Alberta says. "One of my workers is a widow whose husband died suddenly, leaving her with the care of five children." Alberta finds great satisfaction knowing that she is enabling families to make ends meet. Her business has also provided her with numerous opportunities to develop friendships with her neighbors and share the love of Christ with them in a tangible way.

Questions

1. Which of the advantages discussed in this chapter appeal to you most? Why?

2. Is there something you've always dreamed of doing? How can the dream become a reality through your home-based business?

3. Do you think you will have difficulty being your own boss, setting your own hours, etc.? Why or why not?

4. How many hours per week do you plan to work? Write out a tentative work schedule (keep in mind your children's school and nap schedules, etc.).

CHAPTER THREE

Managing Your Time

If you think having four children under age 10 would be enough to keep a mother busy, meet Diane Jensen. After her third child began elementary school, Diane found herself growing lazy and bored, even though she still had a four-year-old at home.

Diane started a home-based cleaning service—not because she needed the money, but because she believes in using her time wisely. Diane's motto is "energy breeds energy," which is why you'll find her out for a brisk walk every morning at six. She then gets the kids ready for school, makes breakfast, and begins her daily chores. All this is in addition to her 20-plus hours of cleaning work outside the home.

Diane thinks the secret to her high energy is her 10-minute afternoon nap. She also has a regular weekly schedule she follows religiously. Her well-organized system enables her to earn extra income and still maintain a busy household.

Unfortunately, most women (especially mothers) are not as organized and energetic as Diane. In fact, when I talk with women about starting a home-based business, one of the most frequent objections I hear is, "I couldn't possibly find the time." Yet many women spend 30 or 40 hours a week away from home and still manage to keep the household running smoothly. This objection points to an underlying fear that they wouldn't get anything done without a boss hovering over them or a production schedule driving them to meet deadlines.

There's little doubt that your business will fail unless you learn to use your time wisely. Working at home provides many distractions and temptations that could pull you away from your business. How effectively you use your time will largely determine how successful your business becomes.

To help inspire you to use your time wisely, I recommend Charles Hummel's outstanding booklet *The Tyranny of the Urgent* (Downers Grove, Ill.: InterVarsity, 1967). In it, he points out:

> When we stop to evaluate, we realize that our dilemma goes deeper than shortage of time; it is basically the problem of priorities. Hard work does not hurt us. We all know what it is to go full speed for long hours,

totally involved in an important task. The resulting weariness is matched by a sense of achievement and joy. Not hard work, but doubt and misgiving produce anxiety as we review a month or year and become oppressed by the pile of unfinished tasks.

Conducting a Time Inventory

I also urge you to conduct a time inventory. This will help you determine how much time you have for a home business and may point out some areas where you can save time. (I have been doing this twice a year since 1982, when I read Michael LeBoeuf's book *Working Smart: How To Accomplish More in Half the Time,* New York, NY: McGraw Hill, 1979.)

Photocopy or re-create the Time Inventory Chart found in chapter 20. Then, for one week, carry the chart with you and jot down how you spend the better part of each half hour (TV, telephone, washing dishes, etc.). But don't suddenly spend two hours in prayer just to make yourself look good. Be honest and try to follow your normal routine as much as possible.

If you're anything like me, this will serve as shock therapy! It may be disconcerting to realize how much of your time is spent on trivial pursuits. Still, the idea is to discern where your time is wasted and strive to recapture it. For me, time flies when I'm on the phone. Like many people, I have a tendency to continue talking long after the usefulness of my words has ceased. If this is an area you struggle with, you may want to keep a close watch on your phone calls as part of your Time Inventory. It might be helpful to set your kitchen clock each time you pick up the phone and, whenever possible, limit your conversation to a predetermined amount of time.

Conquering Time-Wasters

As a self-employed business executive, you can no longer afford to allow time-wasters to control your life. The Bible commands us to "be very careful, then, how you live—not as unwise but as wise, making the most of every opportunity, because the days are evil" (Eph. 5:15-16). The following tips may help you redeem your time:

• Have a daily quiet time. Ironically, one of the best ways to save time is to spend time. Each morning, set aside a quiet time of Scripture reading, reflection, and prayer. This investment will pay rich dividends throughout the day by giving you wisdom to deal with clients and make good decisions.

• Learn to say no. I realize many women, especially Christians, find this difficult. Somehow we have the idea that declining any request for our time and assistance is unspiritual. Nonsense! Jesus did not respond to every request while He walked the earth. In fact, He channeled most of His time and energy into 12 men. Yet He was able to say, "I have brought you glory on earth by completing the

work you gave me to do" (John 17:4). As Charles
Hummel points out, Jesus was able to do so
because "He discerned the Father's will day by
day in a life of prayer. By this means He warded
off the urgent and accomplished the important"
(Hummel, *Tyranny of the Urgent,* p. 8).

In the same manner, we need to be clear about
our calling and purpose. Our top priority, of
course, is our walk with the Lord. And for wives
and mothers, the second priority must be providing
and caring for both the physical and spiritual needs
of our families. Be sure to keep first things first.
Then if you have time and energy to bake five
dozen cookies for the church picnic, terrific. But
don't feel you have to comply with every request
that comes your way. That's a recipe for disaster.

• Don't be a perfectionist. When good enough
is good enough, it's good enough. Is it absolutely
necessary to spend seven hours raking the backyard to remove every last leaf when the yard
looked okay after an hour? Couldn't the dishes
just drip-dry? Do you really have to wipe each
one before you put them away? Maybe I sound
like a sloppy housewife, but the way I see it, life
is too short to waste fussing over minor details.

Remember Parkinson's Law: Work expands
to fill the time available for its completion. It
even expands to fill time that's not available.
Especially when it comes to housework, there's
always more that could be done. I realize this is a
matter of personal preference (and do take your

family's viewpoint into consideration), but strive for balance in this area.

• Stop procrastinating. Again, Charles Hummel says it best: "Unanswered letters, unvisited friends, unwritten articles, and unread books haunt quiet moments when we stop to evaluate" (Hummel, *Tyranny of the Urgent,* p. 3). My most exhausting days are the ones in which I've accomplished the least, because frustration and regret sap all my strength.

If a job needs to be done, it's much better to tackle it and get it over with. Then you'll have the satisfaction of crossing it off your To Do list. If your business is going to succeed, you will have to exercise the "spirit . . . of self-discipline" (2 Tim. 1:7). That means pacing yourself to do a little each day, rather than letting things get out of control before you take action.

• Stop stewing. Most would agree that too much of our precious energy is dissipated in bouts of worry, anger, and bitterness. Don't allow the difficulties of establishing a business to make you anxious. Worry is a waste of time. Pray about the obstacles you're facing, but don't worry about them (see Phil. 4:6-7).

Starting a business requires faith and trust in God's provision, so look at it as an opportunity to grow in these areas. If you find yourself getting discouraged, one of the wisest time investments you can make is memorizing Scripture to counteract negative thought patterns.

• Stop shuffling papers. Paper has a way of invading even the most well-ordered homes. Junk mail, magazines, newspapers, newsletters, and the like are insidious time-wasters. Make it a rule to handle each piece of paper that crosses your desk only once, if at all possible. Act on it, clip it, file it, or throw it away, but don't spend all your time shuffling around the same old papers.

• Tame the telephone and television. These two monsters can wreak havoc on the best-laid plans. Decide how much time you are willing to spend each day on the two Ts and ruthlessly stick to it. If you have a beautiful 20-inch color television with a stereo sound system conveniently sitting in the middle of the living room, it's extremely tempting just to flick the switch (especially if you have remote control).

For years, we kept our black-and-white, 12-inch-screen television in the closet. That way, we had to make a conscious decision to take it out if we wanted to watch it. When we moved to the mountains, we discovered that the only way to get television reception was with a satellite dish. We bypassed the dish, and television simply isn't part of our lives anymore. Just think, all the time you used to devote to watching game shows can now be channeled into your business endeavors. And which will yield greater rewards?

• Schedule shopping trips for off-peak hours and seasons. Shopping for gifts on Christmas Eve is not very wise, nor is grocery shopping on Saturday

afternoon. This is particularly important if your
business will involve shopping for supplies often.
Also, keep those trips to a minimum by maintaining
a list of things you need and buying in bulk.

• Make the most of your waiting time. Rather
than reading the tabloid headlines when you're
standing in line at the grocery store, pull out your
To Do list and bring it up to date, meditate on
Scripture passages, pray, or jot down any brilliant
ideas that come to mind. Do the same while waiting at the dentist's office or bus stop. One of the
best ways to use waiting time, and to manage your
time in general, is by carrying a personal notebook. Remember, your home business will be
only as organized as you are.

Your Personal Notebook

Is your house scattered with little slips of paper
reminding you of things you're supposed to do or
people you have to call? Or worse, is your head
cluttered with thoughts like, *What was I supposed
to do today? What's the deadline for my project?
What time does that meeting start?*

You can get rid of your jumbled thoughts and
scattered notes by transferring everything into a personal notebook. As a home-based businesswoman,
your personal and business lives are intricately
intertwined. A notebook will help balance and organize all the competing demands in your life.

Do important birthdays pass by without a call
or card from you? Your friends will forgive you,

but now that you're a businesswoman, such carelessness may cost you money. That's why the first section of your notebook should be your calendar. Here you will note important events, such as business appointments, deadlines, and meetings, as well as things you need to do.

Your notebook should also include an address section. This will come in handy as you seek to develop your business. For example, someone at church may mention that a cousin needs some typing done. You can jot down his name and number in the address section, then turn to your calendar and write "Call Susan's cousin, Bob Smith." Now that you've got it in your notebook, you don't have to worry about forgetting it or misplacing the information. In fact, you don't even have to think about it anymore; your notebook will remind you.

Do you end up making several trips to the store to pick up things you forgot to put on your list the first time? Create a Shopping List section. Type up a list of all the things you usually buy each week, along with items that should always be in stock. You will probably want to make one list for food and household goods and another for business-related items. Make photocopies for your notebook. Then simply circle the items you need each week.

Your personal notebook will no doubt include individualized sections. I carry the Day Runner Classic Edition, which includes a month-at-a-glance calendar and special forms for daily schedules, business expenses, and a listing of established and prospective clients. An address book is also incorporated into the notebook. In addition, I've inserted tabs and filler paper for recording goals, prayer requests, sermon notes, Sunday school lessons, books to read, and child rearing ideas.

Felice Willat is another woman who believes strongly in the value of carrying a personal notebook. She ought to, since she and her husband founded Day Runner, Inc., one of the most popular personal organizer systems in the world. Day Runner began as a home-based business almost 20 years ago, starting with a small family savings account and lots of friends and relatives. Today, it has more than 1,750 employees and 16 million users around the world. Several years ago, the company "went public," and its stock is now traded on the NASDAQ exchange.

Like so many great ideas, the Day Runner was born out of necessity. Felice was simultaneously working full-time, raising three children, and trying to start her own business. She began carrying a three-ring notebook to keep track of opportunities and information as she sought to juggle her multiple roles. Realizing that many people today—especially women—have to manage a wide range of business, social, and family activities, Felice and her husband converted her notebook into a marketable product.

You will definitely need to purchase a notebook. In addition to the preprinted forms provided, you'll probably want to add customized sections to suit your unique needs. Chapter 20 contains a wide variety of preprinted forms to help you manage your home and business. Simply photocopy those which seem helpful, hole punch, and put them to work for you. (I strongly recommend Anne Ortlund's book *The Disciplines of the Beautiful Woman*, which goes into greater detail about setting up and using a notebook.)

Goal Setting

By far the most important section of any personal notebook should be titled "Goals." I don't mean the resolutions you talk about on New Year's Eve and then forget by January 15. I'm talking about goals that stay with you throughout the year and impact the way you live each day. If you've never set any goals for yourself, now is the time to do so.

Even if it's not January 1 (although that is the ideal time to establish goals), sit down with your notebook, open to the first page of your Goals section, and begin to think and pray about what you want to accomplish with your life. These are your lifetime goals and may include things like "establish a successful home business employing five other women," "write a book," or "provide college tuition for the kids."

Once you have a good idea of what you want to accomplish in your lifetime, determine what you need to do this year to begin making those goals a reality. These constitute your yearly goals and should be more specific. If your lifetime goal is to write a book, your yearly goal may be to write the first five chapters. Or if your lifetime goal is to establish a successful business, this year's goal may be to finish reading this book and decide which business is right for you.

Finally, there are daily goals, which are the most specific of all. In other words, if your lifetime goal is to be a godly woman, and your yearly goal is to read through the Bible, you can do so by reading four or five pages per day. Most of the women I know think they could never find time to read the Bible in one year. It seems overwhelming, but don't you think you could read five pages in one day?

If you want to write a book during your lifetime and plan to write five chapters this year, your daily goal may be to write one page per day. That doesn't sound so hard, does it? That's the advantage of breaking down your goals into manageable tasks: things that looked impossible suddenly seem achievable.

It's important to write out your goals and review them frequently (your notebook makes it easy). The Sabbath is a particularly good day to reflect upon the prior week and evaluate how your time and energy were spent in relation to your goals. The Weekly Evaluation Worksheet at the end of this chapter will assist you through this process.

A time of reflection will help keep your priorities in focus and ensure that you attend to the important, not just the urgent. Should you desire to make use of the Weekly Evaluation Worksheet on a regular basis, a reproducible one is located in chapter 20.

The Fine Art of Delegation

Seventy percent of women surveyed by Ann Landers said they would not raise a family if they could turn back the clock. There is doubtless a variety of reasons why this is so, but I imagine many women are frustrated and exasperated by the incessant work. A lot of mothers feel like slaves to their families, serving as cook, chauffeur, maid, and coach all rolled into one. Unfortunately, many women today feel that they alone must do everything involved with running their households and end up wearing themselves out. That is where delegation comes in.

In view of all you do for your children each day, it is not unreasonable to expect them to contribute to the smooth operation of their own household. Don't underestimate their ability to help out around the house. Even small children can and should be taught to clean up after themselves. Yet how many women spend hours each week picking up after Junior? That's not only bad management, it's bad parenting because it produces irresponsible children. Older children can be given responsibilities including meal preparation, dish washing

gardening, etc. That doesn't mean you turn them
into a band of slaves and render their lives not
worth living. But it does mean instructing children
in the lost art of responsibility. Be sure to make
good use of the preprinted Chore Charts located in
chapter 20.

Mother's Helpers

Even with the assistance of your children,
there may be additional household chores that
should be delegated so you can devote more time
to your business. Proverbs 31:15 says that the
wife of noble character provides "portions for her
servant girls." Most women zip right by this
verse, thinking it's irrelevant to their lives. After
all, who could possibly afford to hire servants?
But I truly believe the concept of "servant girls"
or mother's helpers is an almost universally over-
looked resource for today's busy mothers. I propose hiring a junior or senior high school student
(a girl is usually best) to serve as your special
assistant around the house. She can help out with
baby-sitting, cooking, cleaning, and errands.

Where can you find such an assistant? First, look
to your neighborhood. Perhaps there is a young girl
nearby who would be interested in earning some
extra money (if not, you're living in a very unusual
neighborhood). If you don't have any luck there, try
your church youth group or local school.

Let me urge you to view this arrangement as
more than just a moneymaking opportunity for your

helper and a convenience for you. Young girls yearn for role models, and what an opportunity for you to model the Christian life! You may have a profound, even eternal, influence on her life as you speak wisdom and faithfully instruct her as the Lord leads (see Prov. 31:26). As part of your witness, be sure to give her the "portion" she has earned and encourage her to be a wise steward of her income.

But wait, you may be thinking, *if I have to pay someone to keep an eye on the kids or clean the house, how am I going to make a profit?* If you worked outside your house, you would have to pay someone to watch your children. This arrangement will almost certainly cost you less (I pay between two dollars and five dollars per hour, depending on the job), and you won't have to worry about whether or not your child is receiving good care. And, of course, you'll be immediately available if a problem arises.

For the most part, you will be working side by side as a team. Your helper may be doing the laundry while you work on an article you hope to publish. Or she may play quietly with the children in the backyard while you're on the phone scheduling appointments. I have found this arrangement extremely beneficial. One teenager comes over regularly to help with housecleaning, and a 12-year-old girl frequently plays with my infant daughter while I work on business projects. If my daughter needs me, or if I just want to take a hug break, she's as close as my living room. And because I'm always close at hand, these girls are not only my employees but special friends as well.

In order to make the principle of delegation work for you, bear in mind two basic guidelines. First, be sure to hire good help. If your next-door neighbor is always complaining about how lazy and difficult her daughter is, she's probably the wrong candidate for the job. Second, your assistant will be only as good as the training and tools you provide. Let your assistant know exactly what is expected, and take the time to teach her. Don't just hand her a bucket of cleaning supplies and go your merry way. That's a formula for misunderstanding and is almost guaranteed to generate ill-will on both sides. Training will be time-consuming at first. You'll probably be frustrated by the realization that you could get the job done quicker (and better) yourself. But investing a little extra time now will save you a great deal more in the future.

As you seek to implement these time-saving strategies, realize that you must find a system that works for you. Some of these tips will work for you; others may not. The important thing is realizing that you really do have enough time to establish and operate your own home-based business.

___

TIME MANAGEMENT TIPS

1. Set Annual and Lifetime Goals. What could be worse than coming to the end of your life and realizing you've pursued someone else's dreams? Set your

own goals, then choose a home business that will
enable you to achieve them. Remember: A goal is a
dream with a deadline. Put it in writing. The more
specific, the more likely you are to achieve it.

2. Establish Checkpoints. Researchers surveyed people over the age of 90 and asked them how they
would use their time differently if they could live all
over again. The top three answers: "I would reflect
more," "I would risk more," and "I would do more
significant things." Each week, set aside one hour
to reflect on the activities of the prior week and to
plan the coming week. That way, you can ensure
that you take calculated risks and do significant
things.

3. Carry a Daily Planner. Today's market is flooded
with organizers. Options range from pocketsize to
pocketbooks complete with shoulder straps.
Choose the size that suits your lifestyle. The most
important consideration: Can you carry it with you
at all times? Use your daily calendar to set daily priorities and keep first things first. Ask yourself:
What small thing must I do today to move closer to
my larger goals?

4. Develop Good Habits. Put the power of momentum
on your side. Set up systems for doing routine tasks
in a specific way, at a specific time, in a specific
place. Create "activity centers" for correspondence,
phone calls, accounting, and so on, complete with
all the necessary supplies and equipment. Then you
won't waste time looking for needed items, or wondering what to do, when and how.

5. Apply the 80/20 Rule. Nineteenth-century economist Vilfredo Pareto observed that a small percentage of any activity yields the majority of the results. You will find that 20 percent of your clients comprise 80 percent of your business; 20 percent of your products yield 80 percent of your profit, and so on. Focus your energy on the 20 percent that will do the most good and forget the other 80 percent. You'll actually work *less* and accomplish *more*.

6. Focus. Closely related to the 80/20 rule is the power of *focusing.* Decide exactly what you are in business to do, and focus *all* of your time and energy on becoming the leader in your field. Don't dilute your effectiveness by going in several directions, hoping something will pay off. *Efficiency* is doing things right; *effectiveness* is doing the right thing. It's possible to work efficiently around the clock and never succeed. Work effectively, and you'll achieve your goals.

7. Read *Working Smart* by Dr. Michael LeBoeuf. This is the most influential book I've ever read; it not only changed my approach to time management, it changed my life. A classic must-read for only $5.99. (Call 1-800-759-0190 to order. Note: Written from a secular perspective)

Questions

I. Time Inventory* Once you have completed a week-long Time Inventory in chapter 20, answer the following questions:

1. How and when did I waste time?

2. What activities can be reduced, eliminated, or delegated?

3. Did I attend to the truly important, or merely urgent, things in my life?

4. Does my schedule reflect my priorities?

5. Am I using my time to achieve the goals I've set for myself?

* Adapted from Michael LeBoeuf's *Working Smart: How to Accomplish More in Half the Time.*

6. Whom did I talk to on the phone? Were the calls important and necessary?

7. Did the phone conversations continue beyond necessity? Could they have been shorter and still effective?

II. Weekly Evaluation Worksheet

1. What did I study in my quiet times this week?

2. Which of my business and personal goals did I pursue?

3. Which of my goals did I fail to pursue?

4. Did I attend to important things or merely urgent things?

5. Am I using my unique gifts to develop my business?

6. Am I spending time in my office each day?

7. What specific goals do I have for the coming week?

III. General Questions

1. Indicate below the sections you think you will need for your personal notebook.

2. Make a list of five teenagers you can contact about becoming your helper. If you don't know any prospects, contact your church youth leader.

Assignments

1. Buy and set up your own personal notebook.
2. Set goals.
3. Hire a helper.

CHAPTER FOUR

Your Children and Your Business

Lynn Lentine didn't discover homework — it discovered her. In 1984, Lynn became pregnant with her first child. She had been working for a small construction company for about five years, but business was slowing down. Since the company's facilities were very primitive, the owner didn't think anyone would want to replace Lynn as the bookkeeper. The boss asked Lynn if she would like to work from her home.

Unfortunately, that arrangement didn't last long. She was laid off after a year and forced to find another job. She took another bookkeeping position for two days a week. Concerned about her son's welfare, Lynn drove two hours and 40 minutes every day so she could leave her son with a trusted friend. She knew there had to be a better way to care for her son and keep working.

When a second pregnancy forced her to stay in bed, she offered to do the company payroll from home. It worked out so well that more and more work was sent. This time, the work-at-home arrangement stuck, giving Lynn steady work and the ability to be home with her children.

Today, Lynn provides bookkeeping for two companies. She also works as an at-home supervisor for Christmas Around the World, a home demonstration company. Through this job, Lynn earned a trip to Hawaii for her and her husband, Bob. This year, the entire family is going to Disneyland. That makes it easier for her children, Nick and Alex, to put up with Mommy working!

Lynn's business has grown so much that she can no longer work only at night. She discovered a better way to get things done. Lynn recalls: "It suddenly occurred to me that having a baby-sitter does not necessarily mean Mom is out of the house." So she began hiring teenage girls to occupy the children. That enables her to spend concentrated time working but still be available if needed. Lynn has also learned to work in "snatches" when the kids are napping, in bed for the evening, playing quietly, or watching "Sesame Street" (the great reprieve of mothers everywhere).

Lynn believes that operating a home-based business is the best way to be home with young children and still earn money. However, she warns other women not to think it's easier than working outside the home. "In some ways, it's harder because you're always at the office, yet family and others expect you to be a full-time homemaker," she says. "The key is to realize you are a working mother, even though you don't walk out the door at eight o'clock each morning. Even though it's tough sometimes, I feel like it's the best solution. I'm available for my kids, but I still have the challenge and income that work provides."

Children Benefit When Mom Works at Home

Like Lynn, many work-at-home mothers are realizing the benefits for themselves and their children. The opportunity to spend time with their kids during the preschool years is of prime importance to an increasing number of women. School-age children benefit from having a mother at home as well.

Author Betty Beach surveyed parents about their reasons for wanting to work at home. Beach said: "Interestingly, most parents expressed that their motivation for working at home was to be available to very young children; however, it appears from children's interviews and observations that parental access remains crucial to the relationship long after the preschool years" (*Integrating Work and Family Life,* New York, NY: The State University of New York Press, 1989, 135). Both elementary and high school students were very enthusiastic about having a parent home when they returned from school each day, even if it meant having only a few minutes to recap the day's events. Children derive tremendous security just knowing a parent is available.

Still, some obstacles must be overcome if a mother is going to succeed in a home business. Chief among those obstacles is keeping your children busy so you can get some work done.

Occupying Your Children

One advantage children of working mothers have over those of stay-at-home moms is a greater sense of independence and creativity. When a child only has to say "Mom, I'm bored" (as they so frequently do) and Mom comes running with a book full of games and activities, he really doesn't need to draw upon his own resources very often. When Mom is bored (dare I say it?), she ends up picking up his toys, cleaning his room, and taking care of his chores. As a result, the child may learn to be dependent and irresponsible.

A working mother simply doesn't have time to do these things. And if she's smart, she sees to it that the child takes full responsibility. Believe it or not, I actually remember being jealous of one of my grade-school classmates because her parents were divorced and she lived with her working mother. When she got home each day, she found a note from her mother listing chore assignments. As she finished each item, she crossed it off her list. In return, she received an allowance with which to buy clothes or, best of all, go roller-skating.

It seemed like my life was so dull in comparison. I got home and watched TV while Mom cooked. When I wanted money for roller-skating or clothes, I begged, pouted, and generally acted like a brat until Mom gave in. I now realize the heartache of children from broken homes, but I still admire the sense of responsibility instilled in my childhood friend.

The children of homeworking mothers can have the best of both worlds—an available mom and a strong sense of responsibility. The following are just a few suggestions for balancing the demands of your children and your business. Depending upon the age and temperament of your children, some of the ideas will work; others may not. Experiment with several options, invent your own, and find out how other homeworking mothers cope.

• Establish office hours. It is wise to set aside a specific time each day to work. During that time, post a "Mom Working" sign and instruct the children to play quietly, read, draw, or color. You might let the kids have their own office space, where they can work while you do. Give them paper, crayons, scissors, or if possible, scrap material related to your business, and let them have their own projects just like Mom.

Be sure to establish a tradition of coffee breaks so the kids can look forward to a special time with you. They'll be less likely to interrupt if they know that at 10:30, Mom always spends a half hour with them.

• Work the night shift. When your husband comes home from work, it's DADDY TIME! He can take the kids for bike rides, play games, read stories, and give them their nightly bath while you work. (However, make sure you later have Daddy and *Mommy* time, too!)

• Understand that their sleep time equals your work time. Many women with small ventures find that simply staying up late or waking up early, plus working during naps, provides enough time for a home business. Remember, you can't force your children to *sleep* during nap time, but you can require them to lie quietly on their beds.

• Get some work-time toys. Purchase special toys or videocassettes that can be used *only* while Mom works.

• Use the television—wisely. Of course, TV should never be used as a baby-sitter, but once in a while quality television is okay. Perhaps you can let your youngsters watch public television each morning while you work. If you own a VCR, you can even buy or rent Christian videos, such as the "Adventures in Odyssey" or "McGee & Me" series available from Focus on the Family.

• Create a chore chart. Developing a chore chart is advisable for all mothers but *mandatory* for homeworking mothers. The children can be encouraged to work on their chores during your office hours. In addition to household duties, assign your children jobs related to your home business. When my children wake up each day, they check their "white boards" to get their daily assignments and mark them off as they are completed. (See Dr. James Dobson's book *Dare to Discipline* for further details on assigning chores.)

• Utilize sibling care. If you have both preschool and school-age children, the older children can entertain the younger ones for a period of time each day. You might reward them with a special treat or extra allowance for helping in this way.

• Request Grandma's help. If Grandma thinks it's important for her grandchildren to have a mother at home, ask her to pitch in with some practical help. Even if she can take your children one or two mornings per week, you'll be amazed how much you can get accomplished without distractions.

• Enlist friends and relatives. If you have friends or relatives nearby, particularly with children close in age to your own, they may be willing to help out from time to time. They may agree to watch your children, especially if you can get them excited about your business (offer to keep them in mind when you hit the big time).

In addition to helping me out with free child care, my sister, Helen, is my number-one cheerleader and a great sounding board for ideas. In return, I help her with her nursing school assignments.

• Form play groups. I belong to a weekly play group with eight other moms, so my turn to host rolls around once every other month. On the other seven Thursday mornings, I get two-and-a-half hours of working time, while my daughter enjoys playing with her favorite friends. And it's free!

• Organize a baby-sitting co-op. We have also started a baby-sitting co-op with 30 women. To get started, each member paid five dollars. In return, they received 20 laminated coupons each worth a half-hour of free baby-sitting, plus a list of all the other members. When I need a sitter so I can concentrate on my work, I simply call another mom.

• Set up a baby-sitting exchange. An alternative to a large group is for two homeworking moms to alternate care each week. One Friday, you entertain the children at your house while your friend works at home. The next week, it's her turn. I know a number of women who use this approach successfully.

• Hire a mother's helper. You can hire a pre-adolescent or teenage girl to play with your children while you work. Since you are in the home, you can hire girls as young as 10 to play with your preschoolers. Frankly, I've found the younger girls are much more fun! If your business becomes extremely successful, you can even hire a full-time nanny. Why not think big?

• Let your kids know that playtime's a-comin'. In order for your children to understand your need to work, you need to understand *their* need to play. So take frequent hug-and-fun breaks, and have set times when you put business aside and just flat-out *play*.

• Reward cooperation. When everyone pulls together so Mom can complete her work, it's time for a reward. You don't have to spend all your earnings. Have a day at the park or the beach or in the mountains. You don't have to invest a lot of money—just the time when the children enjoy Mommy's undivided attention.

(For additional ideas, check out my book *No More Lone Ranger Moms,* which provides information on networking with other moms, including strategies for starting baby-sitting co-ops and play groups. Contact Bethany House Publishers at 1-800-328-6109.)

Employing Your Children

As your children watch you carry out the daily tasks of your business, they will come to respect you as a businessperson and as someone whose whole world does not revolve solely around them. Believe it or not, being the center of their parents' world is a heavy load for children to carry. They want Mom to have a life of her own.

The previously cited study conducted by Betty Beach revealed that children of home-based workers were very familiar with the everyday affairs of their parent's business (unlike the average kid, who may only know that Dad works in an office). They were far more informed about the nature of their parent's work than were other children, and most of those interviewed were able to describe actual tasks their parent performed and the tools required.

Beach discovered that children were aware of and involved with the conduct of business in "progressively age-appropriate ways." The four levels of progressive involvement are: play-watch-help; simple tasks; assistance with work on a regular basis; and regular, paid work.[1]

• Play-watch-help. Even very young children demonstrate a keen interest in the activities of their working parents. These youngsters enjoy interrupting their play to observe or help out. At this stage, the child's involvement is strictly spontaneous (for example, a three-year-old might come over and ask if he or she can hold mommy's spool of yarn but will not do so on a consistent or long-term basis).

When my daughter Leah was a toddler, she loved to sit on my lap while I worked on the computer. I had a playpen in my office that I placed her in only when I really needed to concentrate.

• Simple tasks. Young children can be taught to perform simple tasks, such as stuffing envelopes or sorting colored papers. At this stage, helping out should be more fun than work.

Donna Kessel, president of Lynne Designs, allows her two-year-old to open all mail received for her mail-order business. Catherine Smith, proprietor of Cateswear, reports that "work has become a family affair. Two-year-old Kyle is the chief scrap collector and Kris, 13, answers the phones and packs orders."

• Assistance with work on a regular basis, paid or unpaid. As children get older, they can be assigned regular business-related tasks, just as they would be given other household chores. Whether or not you pay your children is a personal decision. Some mothers want to teach their children that everyone should make a contribution to the family, while others feel payment is both a reward and preparation for money management.

Ellen Lane, who runs a sewing school, has incorporated business-related chores into her children's home-school curriculum. In addition, she pays her two oldest children, ages eight and 10, to sweep up material scraps after classes.

Patricia LeBlanc, founder of Hazen Road QuiltWorks, hires her three sons, ages nine, 11 and 15, to package her quilts for mailing. She also pays them to stuff brochures into envelopes. Her three-year-old daughter, Bethany, is also certain to join the QuiltWorks payroll someday. Even at her young age, she is already in charge of removing the safety pins from Mom's finished quilts.

• Regular, paid work. Rather than flipping burgers at McDonald's, your teenager can learn your trade and earn money while preparing for the future. Jean Haven Amos, a real estate agent, hires her teenage daughter, Amy Jo, to distribute a monthly bulletin to houses throughout her territory. Not only is Amy Jo earning money and learning about real estate, she has also learned what it's like to be an employer. To make the work go faster—

and to have more fun—Amy Jo frequently hires friends to help with the flyer distribution. Her mother pays her a set amount per bulletin, and Amy Jo in turn pays her "employees."

Training Them for the Future

Having participated in your business, your children will have a greater knowledge of the business world. They'll also be able to avoid the "Catch 22" most young people face when they're first starting out: You can't get a job without experience, and you can't get experience without a job.

By assisting you with your business, your children will also learn the value of a dollar, and they will better appreciate when their needs are provided—not by some mysterious paycheck but as a direct result of money they've watched you earn by the sweat of your brow. In the words of Linda Cox, who makes stuffed animals, "I think it's good that my work is so visible to my children (ages seven and 11). They understand the relationship between work and home, and they see where the money comes from to pay our bills. Family finances are more realistic to them now."

I agree. I started my home business when I was pregnant with my daughter Leah, who is now nine. So she literally grew up with the business, and I've watched her grow through each of these stages: from watching Mommy from her playpen perspective, to stuffing and licking envelopes, to having her own "home business" selling paintings at my book table when I speak at large conferences around the country.

As mentioned earlier, my "adopted" teenager, Nichole, raised $5,000 for a mission trip with her own home business. At the age of 16, she's already launched a speaking and writing ministry, which she plans to continue as a part-time home business when she gets married someday.

If your business becomes successful, or particularly enjoyable to your children, you may even pass it along to them as an inheritance. Both of my older girls say they want to become writers, just like Mom! What a joy!

Questions

1. Which of the techniques for occupying your children do you plan to implement? How and when will you do so?

2. How can you involve your children in your business? Will they serve as occasional helpers or do you intend for them to become regular employees?

CHAPTER FIVE

Keys to Success

If you've read this far, you are probably quite determined to launch a career as a home-based businesswoman. The perks and benefits sound great—naming your own hours, generating income, being accessible to your children. Still, fear and self-doubt may be holding you back. *I don't have the business smarts,* you may think. *Besides, I have no special abilities or training. How can I go into business for myself? What if I fail?* I assure you, such feelings are quite normal and can be overcome.

You do not need a Harvard Business School degree or an MBA to prosper as an entrepreneur. As a mother, you have accumulated far more skills and abilities than you give yourself credit for. You must rid yourself of the notion that a successful business must be something terribly complex and difficult. Some of the most prosperous businesses are the most simple. And besides, success, like anything else, is in the eye of the beholder.

For you, success may be contributing a few extra dollars to the family budget—or it may be building a full-fledged career. Set your own goals, and when you achieve them, consider yourself a success. But whether you want to establish a Fortune-500 company or just earn an extra 50 dollars a week, there are a few key ingredients that will help you reach your goals. We'll examine 10 elements that will enable you to build a successful business.

Choose a Business You Really Enjoy

Time and time again, home businesses fail because the proprietor selected an endeavor for all the wrong reasons: The woman down the street is starting a typing service, and I can, too. Never mind that you hate to type; there's money to be made and you intend to make it. That, my friend, is a formula for disaster.

Choose a business you can pour your heart into, something you can believe in and feel good about. Consider your talents, interests, and background, and strive to match these to your new venture. You'll enjoy your business more and will be less prone to burn out.

Conduct Thorough Research Before You Begin

Almost all the successful women I interviewed have taken courses on some aspect of running a small business. They have also taken advantage of the free counseling and training services available to them through the Small Business Administration, local university extension services, and similar nonprofit organizations.

Don't be a stranger to the library, either. Read up on your line of business and find out how other people in similar circumstances have succeeded. Also, be sure to learn what competition exists in your area. The more research you do before opening your doors for business, the longer those doors will stay open. (Chapter 21 is filled with information on helpful resources. Be sure to take advantage of all the help available to you.)

Become a Specialist

Imagine this: You've just discovered you have a brain tumor, and the only cure is a delicate surgical procedure. The doctor turns to you and says, "Actually, I'm a podiatrist, but I feel like I can do pretty much anything. Hand me the scalpel." What would you do? You'd run for the door, that's what!

Once upon a time, a doctor was a doctor was a doctor. But this is the age of the *specialist*. People want to deal with the expert in the field. Yet so many home business owners set themselves up as *generalists*. They fall into "the scatter trap"—spreading their energies in a dozen different directions, hoping to hit upon something that clicks.

It'll never work. When you're flying solo, the power lies in *focusing* your energies. What *one thing* gets you out of bed in the morning? What *one thing* are you eminently qualified to do? Focus every ounce of your energies *right there* and forget everything else. If you do, you'll become an expert in your field . . . and business will come to you.

Be Persistent

Your business is not going to succeed overnight. However, if you believe your endeavor is worthwhile and you really want to work from home, all that remains is planning and persistence. In time, you will reap the harvest, but first you must plant the seeds! Don't be content with the current "crop" of clients or your business will soon dry up.

Be willing to invest the time and energy required to continually cultivate future business. Send out flyers to people who have never used your product or service before, and send thank you notes to those who have. Maintain a list of previous customers and mail them a newsletter or updated product list from time to time, just to keep your name fresh in their minds.

Persistence plays a particularly important role in getting started. You may run into obstacles and resistance, and you may be tempted to give up. Knocking on doors and drumming up business day after day can be emotionally and physically tiring. The difference between those who fail and those who succeed often comes down to knocking on one more door.

Discipline Yourself

There's no doubt that self-discipline is critical for success. To some it comes naturally, while others have to work at it. Of course, the degree of self-discipline required varies according to circumstances. A mother of five who works 40 hours a week requires more self-discipline than an empty-nester working 20 hours.

If this is an area you struggle with, *don't let that hold you back*. Go straight out and buy Anne Ortlund's *Disciplines of the Beautiful Woman*. Self-discipline, more than any other characteristic included here, can be learned. Establish accountability with your spouse, partner, or friend, and determine deadlines and checkpoints for progress.

Work Like a Professional

Your image is an extremely important part of your business. Although it's hard to define precisely what is meant by "professional," there are a number of factors that can work together to ensure you make a favorable impression on your associates and clients.

• Your appearance. It's nice that home-based businesswomen don't have to spend a fortune on clothing and grooming supplies. What you wear while working around the house is no one's business but your own. In fact, you can skip the morning makeup madness altogether if you wish. On the other hand, if you want to set an atmosphere to promote work, you may find that wearing a professional-looking outfit is more inspiring than your old bathrobe and fuzzy slippers. On those occasions when you do come in contact with the public, be sure to present the image appropriate to your industry and clientele.

• Your office. If clients or vendors come to your home, your office should be neat, professional, and clearly distinguished from the rest of the house (see chapter 8). If your office can be reached only by passing through the rest of the house, be sure it's clean and orderly before potential clients see it. As much as possible, try to be available during normal business hours.

• Phone manners. Much of your business will probably be conducted over the phone, so make sure you or another responsible adult answers the phone in a professional manner. If your children often use your residence line, it is wise to install a separate business phone unless you can prohibit them from answering the family phone (good luck!). An answering machine or voice messaging service is also a wise investment, enabling you to receive calls when you are away from home. Even if you are home but madness is reigning, it's better not to take the call. You can respond once the household is under control again.

Build a Solid Support System

Over and over again, the women interviewed for this book said one of the keys to their success was a supportive husband, family, and friends. Unfortunately, this is something you have little control over—but you can exert some influence. Long before you put up the "Open for Business" sign, work to win the enthusiastic support of your family and friends. Sell them on your ideas and assure them you are serious about your endeavor.

Once things are under way, you can head off potential conflicts by clarifying expectations. Prior to going into business, you may have taken your child's forgotten book to school or dropped off a report at your husband's office. Make it clear that you remain willing to help in a crisis, but by and large your family shouldn't expect you to do all the things you once did as a full-time housewife. (Balance this with grace and mercy, of course!)

If you are moving from full-time outside employment to a home-based business, make sure your family understands that you're still working—just in a different place. In other words, if you worked at a downtown office from nine to five, would your daughter expect you to drop everything to bring lunch money to school? Of course not. Be very careful here or you can end up with the worst of both worlds: the pressures of a working mother and none of the slack usually afforded to her.

Friends also may have expectations you will no longer be able to fulfill. Perhaps you used to make five dozen brownies from scratch for PTA meetings. Let them know they'll have to settle for store-bought cookies or find another refreshment volunteer. Maybe a special friend is in the habit of dropping in unannounced during the day. She needs to know you're unavailable for socializing during work hours. All of this should be done with tact, of course, so feelings aren't hurt and friendships aren't damaged.

On the positive side, you can enlist the aid of your friends. One of my best friends, Beth Riley, serves as my proofreader. This project has drawn us closer and has built mutual respect.

Cultivate Self-Confidence

When you exude confidence in your skills and services, your customers and clients will be reassured as well. Likewise, if you're unsure about what you have to offer, others are likely to detect this and have the same misgivings.

One way to gain confidence is to do your homework and be fully prepared. Be precise and knowledgeable about every aspect of your business. Know your products, customers, and competition. You can't afford to wing it. Have your spouse or a friend ask you tough questions about your venture. Also, completing the forms at the back of this book and answering the questions at the end of each chapter will help instill confidence, forcing you to think through all the details of launching your business.

You certainly don't need to apologize for being a home-based businesswoman. What you're doing is extremely important. Think of yourself as an exciting trendsetter, paving the way for future generations of mothers.

Learn to Deal Effectively with Others

Your business will inevitably bring you into contact with many new people, including customers, subcontractors, and vendors. Your ability to deal effectively with them will directly affect your success.

Each morning, you should pray over the day's events, the people you are scheduled to meet, and the unexpected interruptions that will occur. Ask God to give you wisdom and grace as you deal with each one.

Be Flexible

Days will come when your son or daughter has a 104-degree temperature. Or perhaps it's sunny and 80 degrees and simply too beautiful not to go to the park. As long as you do not behave irresponsibly (for example, missing a deadline), you can scrap the daily schedule every now and then. You're the boss, so give yourself a day off once in a while.

Flexibility, however, is also necessary to meet the challenges of combining career and family.

You may have to postpone a meeting to take your child to the hospital, or you may be forced to bail out of a family outing to meet a pressing deadline. It's all part of being a home-based entrepreneur!

DON'T FALL FOR WORK-FROM-HOME SCHEMES

1. Beware of any company claiming to offer "Work from Home" opportunities that wants your money up front. Remember, real employers pay you, not vice versa. If a company had a legitimate way for people to work from home, would they have to advertise it? No way! Their current employees would grab the jobs, then tell their family and friends. It would never hit the local want-ads, let alone national newspapers and magazines.

2. If you respond to an ad claiming it can put you in touch with a company looking to hire homeworkers, ask point blank: "Do you have an actual job—not just a list, directory, or plan?" If the answer is no, forget it. Such "lists" are almost invariably useless.

3. Never respond to ads for envelope stuffing. This is an old, old scam. You send them money, then they send you instructions on how to place your own envelope stuffing ad. There are no envelopes to stuff, only chumps to take advantage of. Don't be one of them. By the way, if you play the game, you could go to jail for postal fraud.

4. If it sounds too good to be true, it is, even if you see the ad all the time in legitimate publications. The

company that prominently advertises "Earn thousands with your computer" was just hit with Federal Trade Commission fraud charges and a multimillion-dollar lawsuit. Rule of thumb: Never trust a work-from-home ad (see the rationale under #1).

5. Stop looking for someone to "hire" you to work from home. The chances of that happening are virtually nonexistent, unless you can convince your current employer to let you telecommute. Focus your energies on creating your own business, built upon your skills, interests, and life experience.

TOP 5 REASONS BUSINESSES FAIL . . . AND HOW TO AVOID THEM

1. Our Outdated Educational System. The American education system was founded for one purpose—to train employees to work in the factories of the Industrial Age. It creates, for the most part, people who do what they are told, when and how they are told to do it. Those are vital skills for an assembly line—and some office jobs—but a completely different skill-set (creativity, initiative, multitasking) is required for home business success. So plan to become self-taught . . . or plan to fail.

2. Lack of Marketing Savvy. Who taught you to conduct market research? Target an audience? Develop a "Unique Selling Position"? Deliver a can't-miss sales presentation? No one? That's no surprise. Marketing faux-pas kill countless businesses that could have survived. Become a self-

taught marketing maniac. Read books such as *How to Win Customers and Keep Them for Life* by Dr. Michael LeBoeuf and *Anything* by Jay Conrad Levinson, the *Guerrilla Marketing* expert.

3. Debt. Dun & Bradstreet reports that only 4.6 percent of businesses with under $5,000 of debt fail; a whopping 52.5 percent of businesses with $5,000 to $1,000,000 of debt fail (32.8 percent of those owed less than $25,000). By the way, the statistics for companies using venture capital are not much better. Start small and let your business be self-funding. It's not flashy and it'll take longer, but do you want to be another flash-in-the-pan or a long-term success?

4. Inexperience and Incompetence. The Small Business Adminstration attributes 87 percent of business failure to these two factors. You're bound to make stupid mistakes—wrong product, wrong distribution system, wrong marketing channel, and so on. Would you rather make them on a small or large scale? The advantage of starting a small, self-funding business is this—you make your mistakes on your own dime, when the stakes are manageable. Making adjustments is far more difficult when you have already manufactured $5,000 worth of inventory.

5. Giving Up Too Soon. Dun & Bradstreet reports 53.2 percent of all business failures occur in the first five years. Most were shut down prematurely by skittish bankers, and the rest gave up a week before success

came knocking. View your home business as a way of life, not a particular product or service. When one idea flops, pick another and run with it. Dick Cavett interviewed a panel of millionaire entrepreneurs, searching for common denominators to explain their success. Was it their childhood? No, they had little in common. Was it their education? Nope, they came from various levels of schooling. Was it a particular type of training or job experience? No, that wasn't it either! So what did they have in common? They had each failed in an average of 18 business ventures. Simply put, success means getting up one more time than you fall down!

Home-Based Business Success Evaluation Tool

Not every home business is a smashing success. In fact, some are doomed to failure before they begin. The following evaluation tool will help determine if you're prepared to launch your business.

Rate yourself on a scale of one to 10, with 10 being the highest.

Quality	Rating
You are persistent when the going gets tough	___
You are self-disciplined (no boss is watching you)	___
You are professional (you are your business)	___
You are imaginative (able to go from idea to product)	___
You are courageous and willing to take calculated risks	___
You are patient (it takes time to lay a solid foundation)	___
You are a planner (able to plan ahead)	___
You are self-confident (to carry out your plans)	___
You are resilient (able to bounce back from disappointments)	___
You have selected a business you enjoy	___
You have thoroughly researched your endeavor	___

You have focused on an area where
   you can become a specialist   ____

You have developed a support system
   to encourage you   ____

You have acquired faith to cope with
   financial insecurity   ____

You have a sense of humor   ____

Total   ____

Rating Scale

101 +	What are you waiting for? Go for it!
76–100	Consider yourself most likely to succeed.
51–75	Consider yourself likely to succeed.
26–50	Give it your best shot.
0–25	It's probably not for you.

Part Two

ESSENTIAL DETAILS OF A HOME-BASED BUSINESS

CHAPTER SIX

Laying a Solid Business Foundation

Establishing any business requires both time and money. Before taking another step forward, sit down and honestly evaluate how much of each you are willing and able to invest. This will determine, in large measure, the nature of the business you should undertake.

If you are unwilling to borrow thousands of dollars and risk your home as collateral, don't attempt to launch a nationwide clothing franchise. If you have five children and can't possibly devote 12 hours a day, six days a week, you probably shouldn't open a full-scale catering service. Like anything else in life, it is a matter of trade-offs.

Remember the old saying "nothing ventured, nothing gained"? You will get out of your business whatever you're willing to put into it. No more and no less. Do you envision yourself as a world-renowned entrepreneur? Wonderful. Be prepared to pay the price. On the other hand, maybe you simply need to earn a hundred dollars per week to supplement the family income. That's great, even though you'll never be among the rich and famous. The important thing is to be clear about your priorities.

What Business Is Right for You?

By far the most important decision you have to make is what type of business to launch. Remember, this is a very personal matter, and what's right for someone else isn't necessarily right for you. Don't make the mistake of leaping into an arena that may be totally unsuitable for you just because opportunities exist.

Donna Kessel, founder of Lynne Designs, Inc., started three home-based businesses before finding one she enjoyed. All three failed, because she went into them for the wrong reasons. "I made decisions based on what was convenient and what I had the equipment to do," she says. "I saw other women making money and figured I could do it the same way."

Today, Donna runs a successful mail-order business manufacturing and selling baby bracelets. She has one employee (who works out of her own home) and earns a very respectable salary working just 25 hours per week. Donna strongly urges other women to choose a business they really enjoy: "Do something you've always wanted to do, something you can put your heart into. Don't choose something just to make money."

That's about the best advice anyone can give you. So set aside some time to complete the Skills and Interests Inventory at the end of this chapter. Since being objective about yourself may be difficult, ask your spouse or a friend to complete the Third-Party Analysis Worksheet. By comparing the two evaluations, you will get a good idea of your strengths.

Developing a Business Plan

You've probably heard the saying "Failing to plan is planning to fail." Nowhere is this more true than business. Once you have determined what business is right for you, the next step is writing a business plan. Don't make the mistake of relying on intuition or vague, unwritten objectives. Get your plan in writing.

An important part of being taken seriously is taking yourself and your business seriously. So be sure to take the extra time to produce a plan that is thorough, accurate, and neat. If you plan to remain a one-woman operation forever, it need not be more than a couple of pages. Nevertheless, it's a vital document that indicates to you and all interested parties (financial institutions, insurance agencies, etc.) where you plan to go and how you intend to get there. To help you get started, I've included a Business Plan Worksheet later in this chapter.

Before you set about devising your business plan, take a few minutes to answer the following 10 questions. They will help guide you through the planning process.

1. What do you enjoy doing with your free time? If you enjoy horseback riding, why not become an instructor?

2. Are any of your hobbies or talents marketable? If you're good enough to play piano at church, surely you would be able to offer at least beginner-level lessons. Do you like to cross-stitch? Why not sell some of your projects?

3. Are you imaginative and inventive? How about writing greeting cards? Or are you more detail-oriented and enjoy repetition? In that case, you could serve as a bookkeeper for a local doctor.

4. Do you possess any technical skills? Maybe you worked as a systems analyst before the children were born; why not start a computer consulting business?

5. What do other people say you're good at? What do you think you're good at? If everyone raves about your cooking, consider starting a catering business. Offer cooking lessons in your own kitchen. Have you come up with dessert recipes you know are terrific? Why not bake them and offer them exclusively

through a local, upscale restaurant? *Forbes* magazine recently profiled Debbi Fields, founder of Mrs. Fields, Inc. People liked her chocolate chip cookies so much she went into business at the age of 20. That was in 1977; today her holdings are worth $63 million ("Succeeding By Failing" by Katherine Weisman, *Forbes,* June 25, 1990). Maybe you've got a million-dollar recipe on your hands. You'll never know unless you try.

6. What type of support will be available to you? If you will be working on your own, a modest business venture with minimal investment is best. Perhaps you could do housecleaning two mornings a week. If, on the other hand, you've got a supportive husband and two teenage kids looking to earn extra money, perhaps you can launch an office-services company and get the whole family involved.

7. How much time are you able to devote to your home-based business? A mother with two preschoolers has a lot less free time available than a woman with an empty nest. The first may want to plan children's parties on an occasional basis, whereas the empty-nester will want steadier work, such as a mail-order business.

8. How much money do you want or need to earn? If the family budget is coming up $400 short per month, five haircuts a week ($20

each) will cover it. But if you've made major financial commitments based on two incomes and a baby has just arrived, you had better aim higher.

9. What are some problems you've solved as a mother? What are some gadgets you've come up with to make life easier? Chances are, other mothers are facing similar dilemmas. Think of the person who came up with the "Baby on Board" sign a few years back. How many times did you think to yourself, *I wish people realized I'm driving slowly because the baby is in the car*? A recent craze was glare screens for car windows. Hasn't every mother tried her own techniques for keeping the sun out of her baby's eyes? Someone has to invent these gadgets. Why not you? If you've got an innovative solution to a common problem, why not develop it into a marketable product?

10. Finally, list all the activities you usually do in an ordinary week (grocery shopping, cooking, etc.). Then analyze each area to determine what skills are involved (writing, planning, communication, etc.). What personal qualities (flexibility, self-motivation) enable you to accomplish these tasks successfully? Now, how can you channel those skills and personal qualities into a business venture?

Skills and Interests Inventory

1. List five things you enjoy doing with your free time.

2. List any hobbies or talents you have that may be marketable.

3. What type of temperament do you have: creative or analytical? Meticulous or carefree? Determined or easily discouraged?

4. List any technical or unique skills you possess.

5. List five things other people say you're good at.

6. List five things you think you're good at.

7. What type of support will be available to you?

8. How much money do you want or need to earn?
   Per week ____ Per month ____ Per year ____

9. What are some problems you've solved as a mother? Have you designed some gadgets to make life easier?

10. List all the activities you usually do in an ordinary week in the "Task" column, and indicate the skills involved in the "Skills" column.

Task	**Skills**
_____	_____
_____	_____
_____	_____
_____	_____
_____	_____
_____	_____
_____	_____
_____	_____
_____	_____
_____	_____

11. Based on this information, list 10 possible home-based businesses that might be suitable for you (refer to the list in chapter 19 for inspiration, if necessary).

Third-Party Analysis

Complete the following exercise, evaluating the skills and interests of your friend or spouse. The information will be most helpful if you are as honest as possible.

1. List five things she seems to enjoy doing with her free time.

2. List any hobbies or talents she has that may be marketable.

3. What type of temperament does she have: creative or analytical? Meticulous or carefree? Determined or easily discouraged?

4. List any technical or unique skills she possesses.

5. List five things other people say she is good at.

6. How supportive of a business venture will her friends and family be?

7. How much time do you think she could devote to a home-based business?
Per day _____ Per week _____

8. Based on the above, list five possible home-based businesses that might be suitable.

Business Plan Worksheet

As you continue reading this book, the answers to each of these questions will emerge, so consider your Business Plan a document-in-progress at this point. For now, leave blank any questions you aren't sure about. You should turn here again and again as you move closer to starting a home-based business.

1. Describe the business in detail:
   Company Name: _____
   Address: _____
   _____
   Owner: _____
   Legal Structure: _____
   (Attach copies of legal documents to your business plan.)

2. State the major goals and objectives of the business: _____
   _____
   _____

3. Discuss the special skills and experiences you bring to the company. Describe your qualifications. (Attach a résumé to your business plan.) _____
   _____
   _____
   _____

4. Describe the products or services offered.

_____

_____

_____

_____

5. What advantages do your products or services have over those already on the market?

_____

_____

_____

_____

_____

6. Describe your market (those people most likely to buy your product or service). _____

_____

_____

_____

7. List current customers, if any. _____

_____

_____

_____

_____

8. Indicate when, where, and how you plan to advertise and publicize your business. _____

_____

_____

_____

9. List all equipment and supplies you will require to get started._____

_____

_____

_____

_____

_____

10. Indicate how much money you will need to start. Beside these figures, project how you will obtain it. (Attach a copy of your start-up and first-year budgets.)

Amount   Funding Source

_____   _____

_____   _____

_____   _____

_____   _____

_____   _____

_____   _____

_____   _____

_____   _____

_____   _____

CHAPTER SEVEN

Marketing

Posy Lough, co-founder of The Posy Collection, did her homework before launching her business. Since 1977, Posy has successfully sold Christmas ornaments, handcraft cross-stitch kits, notecards, booklets, and other specialty items.

According to Posy, the secret of her business success is carefully targeting a specific market. She developed products for sale in gift shops in Monticello, Mount Vernon, and Epcot Center. She knew the types of customers these stores catered to, and she targeted them directly. Later, Posy contacted *Focus on the Family* magazine, which ran a brief article on her line of Christian products. The result was thousands of orders and the turning point in Posy's business.

Posy wisely researched who exactly would be interested in buying her products—and then figured out how to present the products to potential customers. To be successful, you must do the same.

First of all, you must identify your "market." In other words, you need to determine which individuals or organizations will want or need your product or service. If your business is making baby bracelets, the people most likely to buy your product are new parents. *The Encyclopedia of Associations* provides customer profiles and industry data by subject and will give you an excellent idea of people who will be interested in your product or service.

This is perhaps the most important step in establishing your business. You may be able to make terrific nose warmers, but if you try to sell them to Hawaiians in July, you're not going to get very far. In order to evaluate the viability of your idea, answer the questions presented at the end of this chapter. You may want to answer them separately for each business you are considering. This process will help you decide which of your ideas are most likely to succeed.

Once you've determined which proposed business is most feasible, you need to develop an effective marketing strategy. Your home-based business will succeed or fail depending upon how carefully you develop a marketing plan. You may offer the greatest service in the history of the world, but if no one has ever heard of your product or service, you won't be in business very long.

Marketing Strategies

Marketing may sound like a complex subject, but actually it's quite simple. Any communication between you and a potential customer is marketing. That includes everything from paid advertisements in newspapers to your business cards. When you send out a letter, the aesthetic impression it makes (quality of the stationery, neatness, and accuracy) is just as important as the actual content. Your company name and logo also communicate volumes, so choose them carefully. The way you answer the telephone and greet people in person also says a great deal about the business you run.

Different industries require different approaches. What will work for a quiltmaker will not work for a secretarial service. I recommend you consult a book specifically geared to marketing in your field (see chapter 22 for a recommended reading list). But, in general, marketing strategies can be divided into three categories: advertising, public relations, and networking.

Advertising

The key to successful paid advertising (and marketing in general) is to keep in mind the four Rs: Marketing must be done at the right time, at the right price, and be presented in the right way to the right people. That's why knowing your market is so important before you invest any money. If you are making a country decor product, advertising in

Time magazine is not a wise choice, but *Country Home* magazine definitely is. Christmas stockings probably won't do very well in June, but advertise the same product in the same place in November, and see what a difference timing makes. Today, a multitude of media exist through which you can reach out to potential customers:

• Newspapers. If your product is general enough to attract a wide audience, advertising in newspapers is a relatively inexpensive way to reach a large number of people in your local area. Newspapers offer both display and classified advertising space. Try to place your advertisement in the section that the most likely buyer is most likely to be reading. For instance, if you are offering cooking classes, place a display ad in the foods section.

• Magazines. Today, magazines are highly specialized. There are magazines for working moms, sports fans, businessmen, exercise buffs, and couch potatoes. Magazine advertising space is more expensive than newspapers, but you can better target the market you want to reach. As a result, the return on your investment may be much greater. Spend some time at a nearby magazine rack or library. Which magazines would be of interest to people who might buy your product? Contact the magazine by letter or telephone and ask them to send you demographics (statistics on who reads their magazines) along with pricing information. This will help you determine where to invest your advertising dollars.

• Radio and television. Advertising on radio and TV can be very expensive. But it can also be very profitable. Although not recommended for the home-based businesswoman on a tight budget, if you have a solid cash flow and have thoroughly investigated the potential return on your investment, you may be ready for this step. If so, consult a professional advertising agency for assistance in developing an ad campaign.

• Direct mail. You probably don't like receiving junk mail, but sending it may prove very profitable for you. This is an effective way of marketing certain types of products. For instance, you wouldn't buy a car through the mail, but you might respond to a limited-time offer to join a book club for your children—especially when you get the first five books for a penny.

Within a week after I brought my baby home from the hospital, the deluge of mail solicitations began. Everyone knew that Mrs. Partow had a new baby. Wouldn't I like portraits taken? How about a personalized bracelet, mug, bib, or diaper bag? Was I interested in receiving a toy once a month? Would I like to join a book club for the baby? You get the picture! And yes, as a new mother, I was interested in some of these things. Where did these people get my name? They bought a mailing list of new mothers.

Direct mail firms across the country offer mailing lists for every category you can imagine. For a price, you can receive a list of everyone who bought a new house within the last few months (so you can try to sell them welcome mats). Again, the key is knowing your market.

Donna Kessel, founder of Lynne Designs, discovered the advantages of direct mail. For a number of years, Donna sold her baby bracelets through retail stores. Although she was successful, that approach involved a lot of running around. Today she pays a fee to a direct mail firm that provides gift packs to new mothers. In return, they place her brochure in the pack, which is distributed to three million new mothers nationwide.

• Yellow Pages. Once you install a separate business telephone line, you are entitled to a listing in the Yellow Pages under the heading of your choice. You are also allowed to purchase a display ad for a modest price. Many entrepreneurs believe a display ad in the yellow pages is the best advertising investment they ever made.

• Flyers. It's Saturday afternoon. Time to go shopping. As you walk through the mall, a young girl hands you a five-by-eight-inch piece of paper. Macy's is having a shoe sale. You come out of the mall and return to your car, only to find that a flyer is lodged under your windshield wiper. You're probably annoyed, but curiosity wins out and you glance at it. You arrive home and a flyer is rolled up in the door handle. Do you read it on the way to the trash can?

The great thing about flyers is the price. You

can write your own and have it photocopied for a modest fee. On the down side, you'll probably have to distribute thousands of them to get any result. But again, keep in mind the four Rs. If you're opening a secretarial service, you may want to visit a nearby college campus to pass out flyers. But handing them out at the grocery store probably wouldn't make sense.

• Word of mouth. The best form of advertising in the world is word of mouth, and the only way to get it is to earn it. Treat your customers right. Provide them with top-notch service or merchandise in a timely and courteous fashion, and the customers will come to you.

Public Relations

Simply said, public relations is anything that gets your name before the public. This may involve providing services or products in return for goodwill, and hopefully, future business. When you donate 10 dozen cookies to the local fair, carefully wrapped and clearly labeled "Sharon's Cookies," that's good public relations. Everyone thinks you're an incredibly nice person for giving away free cookies—and if they like them, they may become paying customers.

If you own a furniture rental business, you could lend several pieces for a local college theater production in exchange for a mention in the program. Or you may help sponsor a free blood-pressure screening at the local mall. In return,

your business name might be included in promotional ads or posters.

An important component of public relations is
publicity. This is exposure provided by the media,
free of charge. Understand that publicity is only
granted when it's in the media's best interest, not
yours. *The New York Times* is not going to write a
story about you so you can sell more of your
homemade WWJD bracelets. But they might run
the story as part of an examination of current
trends in youth culture. Remember that there are
many different sides to any story (mothers know
all about that, right?). Be sure to slant yours
accordingly.

When you seek publicity, present your story in
terms that will interest the newspaper or magazine's editorial staff. Is your product truly intriguing or unique? Is it designed to meet an emerging
need? Does it reveal something about your community or the country at large? For example, my
sister-in-law lives in a community that, for hundreds of years, was predominantly Amish. She is
offering a catering service, which is obviously not
of interest to the Amish. However, the community has been deluged with Yuppies over the past
decade. A catering service is not interesting news;
the fact that Yuppies are flocking to the country is.
The first angle would not yield publicity; the second very well might.

Carefully examine newspapers and magazines
in which you would like to obtain coverage.

Determine what types of stories they run and in which sections of the paper or magazine you might fit. Most major papers have a Lifestyles section, as well as Metro and Business sections, and the ever-popular Food section. Target the section in which you would like to appear and tailor your approach accordingly.

Once you obtain publicity, make the most of it. Quote commentary in your brochures (for example,"'Fabulous' says *The Miami Herald*" or "*The Chicago Tribune* calls it the 'Best buy west of the Mississippi'"). Photocopy the article and include it in your promotional materials. It's always eas-ier to let someone else do the bragging for you! If you manage to get an entire article devoted to you, make reprints and distribute them to everyone on your mailing list.

• Press releases. Call the local newspaper and find out what its criteria are for news releases. If you've been in business for three years and are simply looking for press coverage, don't count on it. But if you're just starting out or branching into new areas, especially if you offer a service to the general public, newspapers are often responsive. A news release is usually a straightforward, one-page story or description about an event or product. It has the tone of a news article, with few flowery adjectives.

Compose a release and mail it to the appropriate editor, along with a cover letter, black-and-white photos of you or your product, and samples, where appropriate (who wouldn't love to receive free brownies?).

Here, according to editors, are the top 10 reasons why a news release is likely to end up in the trash:

1. It's poorly written.
2. It sounds like advertising copy.
3. The subject is not suitable for the publication.
4. It doesn't contain enough information.
5. It's too long. (See #1.)
6. It's too technical for the publication and the readers.
7. The writing style doesn't fit the publication.
8. The information is irrelevant or uninteresting. The story has no "local" angle.
9. The photographs or graphics are not up to the standard of the publication.
10. The information is "old news" or it arrives too close to the editorial deadline.

If you avoid the top 10 ways to land your press release in the trash can, you might just land on the front page!

• Promotions. A promotion is any special event you host to publicize your business, such as a grand opening, party, open house, or participation in large-scale events. The key to successful promotions is assuring everyone that free food and prizes will be on hand. The lure of freebies may garner some publicity for your business.

• Seminars and workshops. Contact local adult

education programs in your area and indicate your availability and credentials to present workshops and seminars. You might also offer to speak for local community groups, free of charge if necessary. Remember, in these contexts, you will be selling yourself and your knowledge, not necessarily your product or service. But you will receive exposure and the hope for future business.

When I was first getting started, I made a phone call to the local school district's continuing education program and indicated my availability to conduct evening workshops on working at home. As it turned out, they were very interested. I taught several classes, enabling me to earn a respectable hourly income while providing me with additional exposure to the community.

• Talk shows. Getting on "Good Morning America" may be beyond your reach (then again, remember Marcia Cone-Esaki from chapter 1?). But local television and radio stations run talk shows on a daily basis. Did you ever stop to think where they find guests, day after day? How are those guests selected? Station managers or other staff are paid to find experts and interesting people. Just think what a great favor you'll be doing them by offering to lend your presence to their show. If you have something interesting to say and are able to express yourself well, go for it!

"Fifteen minutes on the radio revolutionized my business," say Rhonda Anderson of St. Cloud, Minnesota, founder of Creative Memories. She is referring to her appearance on Focus on the Family, the second-largest nationally syndicated radio show in America, with several million listeners. "I knew the show reached my target audience—homemakers. So I hoped to generate interest in my program. It took five months of letters and phone calls—and a personal visit to the show's producer in California—before I finally got on the program. My efforts were well rewarded, though. As a direct result of the program, we received more than 7,000 calls and recruited 600 women." Today, her modest home business has become a multimillion dollar business.

Radio talk shows present an excellent opportunity for you to promote your home-based business, whether you market a product or serve as a consultant. There are 1,000 radio talk shows in America, requiring an estimated 1 million guests per year. Although "Larry King Live" probably won't invite you to appear, you can still make the airwaves into an effective marketing tool.

Here are some tips for getting on the air:

• Identify. Determine which shows' content is aimed at your prospects. There are programs for sports buffs, animal lovers, political conservatives, and every other demographic you can imagine. Check out the *Annual Broadcasting Yearbook* ($179; 1-800-521-8110), the who's who of the radio industry. (Try your library before you shell out your own money.)

• Tune in. Before you pick up the phone to

book your first radio interview, listen to your targeted programs to discover their unique style, including the host's personality and philosophy. With this information in mind, you'll be better able to "pitch" yourself as a desirable guest.

• Contact the producer by phone. Don't bother the host; he or she is not interested. Briefly explain how your topic will meet the audience's needs. Realize the producer is screening you on the spot, so know exactly what you want to say.

• Prepare a media kit. Within 24 hours after your initial contact, send your publicity materials, including a cover letter (describing how interviewing you will benefit the listener), an outline of your suggested program topics, with questions the interviewer may wish to ask. (Many hosts will use your list verbatim.) Also include a press release or article describing your product or service and your professional biography. A "quote sheet" filled with endorsements is especially helpful, as are article reprints.

• Follow up. Don't expect the producer to contact you. Take the initiative. Be persistent, but don't be a pest. (Where you cross that line depends on your personality and the producer's patience.)

• Capitalize. Make the most of your time on the air. Offer listeners a way to respond. Give an 800 number for listeners to call. If the show objects, ask if you can offer a free tip sheet or informational booklet. Most hosts encourage freebies because listeners love them.

• Parlay. The first interview is the hardest to obtain. Once you've proven your ability to perform on the air, you can parlay one appearance into dozens more. The power of radio happens when you become a "regularly featured guest" on a variety of programs. With each show you book, the next one becomes a little easier. You might consider advertising your availability as a guest in *Radio-TV Interview Report,* a bimonthly magazine distributed free to 3,800 talk-show producers (call 1-800-989-1400). The cost is about $350 and up.

• Read all about it. Pick up a copy of *On the Air: How to Get on Radio and TV Talk Shows* by Al Parinello (1-800-CAREER-1). As the title implies, the author teaches you exactly how to get on talk shows and, more importantly, what to do when you get there. The book also includes a contact list with more than 800 local and national talk shows. For $12.95, it's a very valuable guide.

Be sure to express your appreciation to those individuals who provide publicity. Send a thank you note. Building relationships with local media personnel can certainly increase your chances of receiving additional coverage in the future. And everyone appreciates a little kindness.

Networking

Networking involves making specific plans to meet people who can provide you with personal and professional support, useful information, and business. When you think of establishing a network, first look to your current circle of friends and business associates. Many of them probably can and will be of service in numerous ways. Perhaps your cousin Bob is a computer salesman. He can give you advice and, hopefully, a great discount. Your former boss might be willing to hire you as a subcontractor when the office is short-handed. Maybe your next-door neighbor is on the staff of the local newspaper; she may help you get some publicity.

Your current contacts are, more than likely, not sufficient. Like it or not, when it comes to business, who you know is often more important than what you know. (Be honest now—wouldn't you rather do business with someone you know, rather than a total stranger?) So try to get to know as many people as possible. Consider joining organizations such as the local chamber of commerce. Attend seminars and workshops geared to small-business owners or others who may be able to use your service or product.

Trade associations exist for many different fields, such as the American Bar Association, the National Association of Secretarial Services, and hundreds of others. There's bound to be one related to your business. Joining will give you the opportunity to meet people who have faced similar struggles and can provide valuable advice. For a list of associations related to your industry, check out *The Encyclopedia of Associations,* available at your local library.

You may even find that elusive but desirable individual known as a mentor. That's someone who not only has been down the road you're traveling but is willing to share experiences and help you along the way.

Wherever you go, be sure to carry business cards and hand them out liberally. These are small enough that most people are willing to save them, whereas they might toss a brochure or advertisement. And be sure to ask for business cards from people who might be future business associates.

Your notebook (see chapter 3) should contain a section titled "Contacts and Prospects," where you can record the name and address of new contacts you make. You should also have a place to retain business cards. Stationery stores sell special files to hold business cards. You may simply keep them in a small box or staple them onto address cards.

Speak Up for Your Business

One of the most valuable skills a home business owner can possess is the ability to speak up for his or her business. Whether you are making a one-on-one presentation to a potential client, offering seminars to promote your business, or speaking to the local Rotary Club to get your name out, the ability to state your case persuasively is absolutely crucial. The surest route to home business success is establishing yourself as an expert or leader in your field. Once you have done so, the onerous task of marketing becomes simple. Business will come to you.

If you want people to beat a path to your door, the surest route to take is polishing your presentation skills. You can then parlay those skills into information products that cost virtually nothing to develop but yield rich dividends. This is the Information Age. It doesn't matter if your primary business involves a product or a service, information products can enhance your bottom line with minimal investment. Among those information products might be a full-day seminar, a half-hour presentation, audiocassettes, even a self-published book or booklet transcribed from taped presentations.

Another bonus of learning to speak up for your business is that once you are skilled enough, you actually *get paid* to market yourself. That's right! Organizations will pay you to talk to audiences filled with your potential customers. When it comes time for these prospects to decide whose product or service to buy, who do you think they will choose? The guy sitting next to them . . . or the person behind the microphone? The answer is obvious.

So don't just sit there all alone in your home office. Get out there and speak up for your business. Here's how:

• Read. Discover how to develop your speaking skills and put together speeches and seminars related to your business. Check out my favorite,

Inspire Any Audience by Tony Jeary ($14.95; call 1-800-678-8014, ext. 200). It covers everything from preparing your presentation to overcoming nervous jitters, from using tools effectively (flip charts, overheads, handouts) to getting your audience to take action. Every home business owner should own this book. The material is also available on audio and video (for more information, call 1-800-982-2509).

• Listen. Nightingale-Conant offers several audiocassette programs designed to accelerate the learning curve for aspiring speakers. One of the best is *Creating a Powerful Presence: How to Get Your Message Across with Clarity, Focus and Power* by Bert Decker, a six-cassette program ($59.95; call 1-800-525-9000). Check out the company's on-line catalog at www.nightingale.com.

• Learn. Join organizations that can take you to the next level. Check out some of the following:

Toastmasters International
P.O. Box 9052
Mission Viejo, CA 92690
(714) 858-8255
www.toastmasters.org

This is the world's largest organization devoted to communication excellence. Through local clubs, Toastmasters offers you the opportunity to learn—and practice—speaking skills. Clubs meet weekly and are located in most communities in America.

National Speakers Association
3877 Seventh Street
Suite 350
Phoenix, AZ 85014
(602) 265-1001
www.nsaspeaker.org

A professional association with chapters in most major cities, NSA offers a fabulous national convention, as well as regional and local meetings, designed to hone speaking skills for the serious professional.

CLASServices, Inc.
P.O. Box 66810
Albuquerque, NM 87193
(505) 899-4283
1-800-433-6633
www.classervices.com

If you are interested in communicating to Christian audiences, contact Marita Littauer. Marita's ministry is called CLASS, which trains others to succeed as Christian communicators. Whether you want to speak, write, or both, Marita can help. Her three-day training program, called the CLASS Seminar, was absolutely life-changing for me. She also offers training via books, audiocassettes, and videos. In particular, I'd encourage you to order a copy of her book *Talking So People Will Listen,* which presents much of the CLASS Seminar material in book form.

Checking Out the Competition

A discussion of marketing is not complete without considering the number-one obstacle your business must overcome: competition. More than likely, your business will not be entirely unique. That means you will have to deal with competition, so find out all you can about your competitors before you open for business.

First, look in the Yellow Pages to find similar businesses. Also, scan newspaper ads and keep your eyes open for flyers and direct mail pieces. If you find competitors, call and ask questions, and request brochures and other material. This information will help you find your own niche in the marketplace.

If you believe you can realistically compete or there is enough business to go around, then you should proceed with your marketing plans. If not, consider some other possibilities until you find your niche.

Pricing Is a Marketing Decision:
For Cheaper or For Best?

Nothing strikes fear into the heart of the home-worker like the issue of price. How do I know what my products are worth? How much should I charge for my services? And all too frequently the answer is, "I'll charge less than the competition."

But stop and think. Do you really want people

to buy your products just because they're the cheapest? How will you feel providing a service to someone who hired you only because he thought he was getting a bargain? Cheaper is not always better. In fact, when it comes to home businesses, I'd say cheaper is almost always worse.

Charlie Dunn worked on an assembly line stitching boots for little better than minimum wage. Eventually, those boots made their way into stores where they sold for about $100 a pair. But one day he looked in the mirror and decided he was worth more. So he launched his own business making customized boots by hand. Did he sell his boots for $50? Not on your life. He made boots to sell for thousands of dollars per pair. He made boots for Ronald Reagan, Clint Eastwood, even the Pope. Country-western star Waylon Jennings loved Charlie's boots so much, he wrote a song about them.

Same man. Same product. What made the difference? He set his sights not on being the cheapest, but on being the best. How about you? As you consider what your products or services are worth, will you settle for being cheaper? Or will you strive to be the best?

How to Price a Product

Too many home business owners don't pay themselves a decent wage. Don't make that mistake. Instead, use the following formula to establish a fair price:

1. Decide what is the minimum wage you are willing to work for: _____
2. Calculate the time invested in each product.
3. Calculate your material costs.
4. Minimum price you need to charge is 1 x 2 + 3.
5. Evaluate the market. Can you get your price? If not, *don't* lower the price. Instead, choose another product.

   Let me give you an example. Suppose:

1. You are willing to work for $5 per hour.
2. It takes you five hours to make each product.
3. Your materials cost $20.

   You would have to charge $5 x 5 hours ($25) + 20 = $45.

How to Price a Service

Asking price equals perceived value. Too many home business owners undercharge, hoping to gain a competitive advantage. It'll never work. Charge what you're worth and be worth what you charge. Research the annual salary for an employee performing comparable work. Then add on your estimated operating expenses for the year. Divide the total by 50 weeks per year, then by 40 hours per week. That's how much you need to *pay yourself.* But since you won't be able to bill every hour that you work, bill your client at least *twice* that amount.

Top 10 Marketing Strategies

1. Develop a Unique Selling Proposition (USP). Get

this one right, and the rest of your marketing will be a breeze. Come up with a totally unique product or service—or just a unique delivery system (Dell offered the first "mail order" computers) or unique style (Mary Kay's pink Cadillacs). Deliver superior quality with a novel, even unconventional, twist and people may well buy just because they remember you. Whatever it takes!

2. Pursue Tie-Ins. *The Wall Street Journal* says your toughest obstacle is overcoming suspicion. People don't trust strangers and that's what you are until your business is well established. To overcome this obstacle and gain instant credibility, "tie in" with a respected business. For example, I often tie in with large organizations to offer my Home Business Workshop. I've tied in with the CIA (yep, the CIA!), senators, governors, and various Christian organizations. They market the event under their name, thus attracting a larger audience. In some cases, I was paid a set fee; other times I received a per-attendee price. On other occasions, I agreed to share whatever profit the event generated. Even though I had to share the profits, I still came out ahead because there was a lot more to share.

3. Send Out Press Releases. Write one- to two-page "mini-articles" or "notices" about your business and send them to magazines and newspapers read by your target audience. Researchers studied an issue of *The Wall Street Journal* and discovered 50 percent of articles were based on press releases; of those, 53 percent ran word for word. Newsworthy

topics include: commenting on trends, offering practical tips, announcing start-up and business anniversaries, major clients landed, upcoming speeches or seminars. Read *Do-It-Yourself Publicity* by David Ramicitti.

4. Offer Free Booklets. Self-publish an informative booklet related to your product or service, packed with valuable advice and helpful hints (not just a sales pitch). On the last page, include an order form or response card. Send press releases to magazines and newspapers read by your potential customers, offering the free booklet in return for a self-addressed stamped envelope or $1 to cover shipping and handling. If you've targeted your market right, you'll have an instant mailing list of potential customers.

5. Plant Seeds. The cheapest and most effective marketing is word-of-mouth—and some mouths are worth more than others! Who are the trend-setters, opinion shapers, authorities, and celebrities in your industry? Folks like magazine and newspaper columnists, radio and TV hosts, club presidents, and civic leaders. Identify someone who can authoritatively spread the word, then plant a seed by giving him or her a free taste of your business. Plant your seeds, then watch them grow!

6. Give Speeches and Seminars. All business owners need to know how to speak up for their business. There are few marketing strategies as cost-effective as standing in front of a captive audience

filled with potential customers, demonstrating your brilliance. (Get good enough and you'll even get paid to do it!) Join Toastmasters, a non-profit club where you can refine your speaking skills at weekly meetings.

7. Get Booked on Radio and TV Shows. More than 1,000 shows require one million guests per year—the opportunities are incredible! There's a whole lot of air-time to fill, so why not wax eloquent about your industry? Some shows will even let you promote your business, but be sure to get permission first. If you can't, offer a free booklet to build your mailing list. A toll-free number is a real plus.

8. Network. Cultivate contacts for personal support, information, professional advice, referrals and, of course, new business. Network with former colleagues and at Rotary Clubs, Chambers of Commerce, and online communities. Set a goal to tell someone new about your business every day. Have plenty of brochures and business cards handy. Then live by the motto: Do unto others as you'd have them do to you.

9. Consider Multilevel Marketing. Although crooked MLMs have given the industry a bad name, building a legitimate MLM to sell your products is a super marketing strategy. Begin by developing a great line of unique, quality products that you can market using a "home party" or "seminar" approach. Refine your sales presentation, then teach it to others, who can teach it to others.

You'll probably need an attorney to prepare a commission structure and distributor contracts.

10. Write a Book. If you offer a service, nothing enhances credibility like authoring a book that showcases your knowledge of the industry. Suddenly, you are an expert in the field, and clients start coming to you. Hundreds of publishers release 55,000-plus books per year, so opportunities abound. If you're truly adventurous, you can even self-publish.

Questions

1. Is your product or service something people use all the time? Is it practical?

2. If people are not currently using it, can you convince them they ought to? How?

3. Describe the person most likely to buy your product or service.

4. What magazines are your potential customers likely to read? (Look at the *Reader's Guide to Periodical Literature* at your local library or simply peruse a magazine rack for inspiration.)

5. Is your product or service general enough to warrant advertising in the local newspapers? If yes, list those newspapers you plan to contact for advertising information.

6. Where and how have you seen similar products advertised? Begin clipping and filing all competitive ads.

7. Is your product or service the type that would be promoted through a direct mail letter or flyer? If so, develop a sample letter advertising

your product. Get feedback from your friends
and relatives.

8. Who are your competitors?

9. In what ways are their businesses similar to
   yours?

10. How will your service or product be better?

11. Do their businesses seem to be growing or declining? Why?

12. Assuming you can offer a competitive product or service, can you do so at a price that makes your effort worthwhile?

Questions About Publicity

1. What is interesting or unique about your product or service?

2. Does your product or service reveal anything about your community or our society?

3. What newspapers and magazines would you like to be featured in? List them under "Publication." Obtain several copies of each and study them to determine which section you might fit into and the name of the appropriate editor or reporter to contact.

Publication	Section	Contact
_____	_____	_____
_____	_____	_____
_____	_____	_____
_____	_____	_____
_____	_____	_____
_____	_____	_____

4. List five ideas for promotional events.

5. List 10 friends, relatives, or former colleagues who may be able to help you, and how.

6. List two local organizations you might consider joining for networking purposes.
   Contact each to obtain more information.

7. Review the list of associations in chapter 21.
   List those you will contact for more information.

Assignments
1. Write a press release.
2. Have photos taken of you and your product, if
   appropriate.
3. Find out if your community offers an adult
   school and if they would be interested in having you teach a class.

CHAPTER EIGHT

Your Home Office

One of the first requirements for a home-based business is finding a place to work. Ideally, you should have a room set aside expressly for this purpose, but of course, that is not always possible. But don't be dismayed; be creative. When I was a student, my husband and I were living in a small one-bedroom apartment, and a quiet work space was mandatory. Believe it or not, I set up a little desk table in a closet and used it as my office! Actually, this arrangement worked surprisingly well because I only went in there when I was serious about working. That is one of the most important rules of a good office: Use it only for working. That way, you will learn to associate your office with productivity.

Your office may simply be a section of your bedroom or living room set aside exclusively for your use. Perhaps you could fashion a partition to make things look more official. If you take your business seriously, your family and friends will be more inclined to respect your efforts.

Search flea markets if you must (a friend of mine bought a beautiful desk with a typing stand for $7.50 at an auction) in order to set up the basics of an office: a table and chair, calculator, pencil cup, stapler, paper clips, in-out trays, and so on.

The best way to keep organized is to create a place for everything. It sounds hackneyed, but it really is much easier to keep things in place that way. Don't clutter your work area with photographs and knick-knacks; put the former on the wall and sell the latter at a yard sale! Strive for a professional appearance.

You should also give careful attention to which colors you select for your office. Research demonstrates that colors actually have a physical affect on the human body. Red, for example, increases blood pressure and is associated with energy and stimulation. So if you need a boost to get going, buy some red cloth for curtains, a wall-hanging, or whatever. Yellow is a bright, cheerful color, so you may want splashes of yellow in your work area—a dried flower arrangement, tablecloth, etc.

If you tend to be hyperactive and your work requires a relaxed frame of mind, blue and green are associated with reduced blood pressure, relaxation and tranquility. My carpet and desk are both light blue.

Avoid blacks, browns, grays, and earth tones. These are not only associated with fatigue and sedate behavior but actually make the available space seem smaller. White, on the other hand, is a neutral color that increases the perception of space. It's hard to go wrong with white or off-white walls. By the way, any money you spend fixing up your office is completely tax deductible (see chapter 12).

Once you've established your office, all that remains is to make good use of it. One very practical approach is to hold office hours during the same time each day, if at all possible. During this time, the family knows not to disturb you unless something urgent comes up. Your office hours may be before the children wake up, during nap time, or after they are in bed at night. Or you may train the children to read, do homework, or play quietly during your work hours.

Try to maintain a log to record the date, number of hours worked, and the project you worked on. When the time comes to bill clients or price your products, this will provide a basis for calculating costs. The important thing is that you work a little each day, rather than allowing projects to accumulate. And again, only sit in your office when you want to work.

Your Desk

You will be spending many hours at your desk, so it pays to invest some thought and planning into making it right from the start. Purchase the most comfortable desk and chair you can afford. If you're a mother, you have enough things wearing you down without having to endure back and neck strain from working in an uncomfortable position. Your increased efficiency will pay for the desk several times over.

As with your office in general, avoid clutter on your desk. As a rule of thumb, if you don't use an item at least once a day, it doesn't belong on top of your desk. Staplers, tape dispensers, and the like are wonderful gadgets, but if all they do is occupy space, let them be wonderful in a drawer somewhere.

I recently hosted a small church retreat at my home. The women were amazed when they saw my desk—but not because they were impressed by its grandeur and beauty. Quite the opposite! For more than 10 years, I have worked at the same tiny desk (remember, it had to fit in my three-foot wide closet-office!). It became my desk when a friend was throwing it out because it was so old and beat-up! Every so often, my husband suggests I buy a new desk. He says my dinky, rickety old one is an eyesore. I don't care! This little desk has been with me through the launching of my business and the writing of seven books. So as long as it keeps standing, I'll keep it around.

The moral of the story? Your desk doesn't have to qualify for the cover of *Office Beautiful;* it just has to work for you.

Essential Equipment

The equipment you require will depend upon the type of business you have. A clown company probably can't get by without a helium-balloon dispenser, a dog breeder will need to purchase cages, and a free-lance photographer will want darkroom equipment. But certain equipment will benefit virtually any business.

• Telephone. There are several reasons you may want to consider installing a separate business telephone line. First, doing so enables you to list your business in the Yellow Pages, which is an important advertising medium. Second, if you or your children frequently surf the Internet, you may never be able to make phone calls if you have only one line. (I have a teenager, so I know about this problem!) Third, when the phone rings, you can be sure it is business-related and answer the call appropriately. If you have children, you can instruct them not to answer your business phone (older children may be an exception). Fourth, you can avoid publicizing your home phone number on business cards, advertisements, and brochures.

Today, phone companies offer a wide variety of services that may be beneficial. If your business receives a high volume of incoming calls, you may want to install call waiting. You may even want to invest in several lines, with a hold button, if warranted. Customers who are met with a busy signal or continuous ringing are likely to take their business elsewhere. Remember, saving money in the short run may cost you in the long run.

Another option worth considering is "distinctive ringing," which typically costs $10 per month. Here's how the service works: The phone company assigns a second phone number to your existing phone line. When a caller dials the second number, you hear a double ring. The advantage of distinctive ringing is that it's much cheaper than installing and maintaining a second line. I used this option for many years, and it worked quite well. My children knew not to pick up the phone when they hear that double ring.

• Answering machine or voice messaging. I had initially planned to eliminate this section on answering machines, thinking they were obsolete. Then I discovered that voice mail service doesn't reach the small mountain community I recently moved to. Much to my amazement, I was suddenly transported back to the Stone Age of answering machines. Voice messaging is obviously the best option, but those of you, like me, who live in rural areas will have to make do until technology reaches the hinterlands.

Answering machines can be purchased for under $50 and are well worth the investment if incoming calls constitute a major avenue of business development. If you have commitments that require you to be away from home for long periods of time, you can't afford not to purchase one. The advantage of voice messaging is that your callers can get through and leave their message even when you're on the line. As a result, there's no such thing as a busy signal.

• Computer. Personal computers are becoming as commonplace in American homes as televisions. In our home, we have one rarely used television and two constantly used computers! They can enhance both your efficiency and professional image. Of course, the nature of your business will determine whether you need a computer. (See chapter 9 for a complete discussion.)

• Typewriter. In many cases, computers have rendered the typewriter obsolete (it's still easier to type an envelope, though). Depending on your business, however, a typewriter may be sufficient. Or if you cannot afford a computer, you may want to obtain an electronic typewriter (they are fairly easy to come by secondhand). All correspondence sent out from your home office should be typed. In the long run, typing it yourself will save you money.

• Filing cabinet. No matter what line of business you enter, paper is bound to flow in and out of your office. Government forms, financial records, customer information, and invoices all need to be retained in an orderly fashion. Fireproof metal cabinets are a wise investment, but they can be expensive. Again, you may find one secondhand. In the meantime, you can use cardboard filing boxes or heavy plastic containers, available at any stationery store.

Organizing a Filing System

As a general rule, try to throw away more than you file, otherwise you'll drown in a sea of paper. Only save what you really need. For example, don't save an entire magazine; save only the article of interest to you. Of course, some things will certainly need to be saved for retrieval at a later time. Some suggested file categories are listed below.

• Subject file. The best way to set up your initial subject files, according to Robert Scott, author of *Office at Home*, is by labeling a series of file folders A-Miscellaneous through Z-Miscellaneous. That way, you can create specific subject files as warranted. For instance, once your G-Miscellaneous file has accumulated five letters from George's Paper Supply, you can make a subject file especially for it.

Another approach is to set up temporary files by marking folders in pencil or by attaching a Post-It note. Affix a typed label only when you are certain you need a file for that particular subject. It doesn't make sense to make a separate file for every piece of paper you want to keep. If you do, you'll have 100 files within a few weeks.

Eventually, you should have a file (by company or individual name) for every major customer or vendor you do business with. You should also make subject files for special projects you are working on or topics that relate to your business. For example, you may be developing a new product line to add to your mail-order business. Make a special file and put everything pertaining to it in one place (regardless of who the vendor is). Or you may hope to write a book someday on child rearing. If you come across helpful articles from time to time, file them all in one subject folder, rather than by author or some other means.

File folders and labels are both available in a wide variety of colors, so you may consider color-coding your system. For example, vendors may be in yellow folders, clients in blue folders, projects in green folders, and so on. Alternatively, you may opt to use all manila folders with different colored labels.

• Chronological file. You should maintain a copy of all correspondence sent out from your office in date order. The best approach is to three-hole punch each document and store it in a binder. Once the binder is full, mark the beginning and ending dates on the side of the binder and start a new one.

• Tickler file. These files are designed to bring papers to your attention when needed, no sooner and no later. There are two primary methods for this. The first is a folder or binder with index tabs numbered one through 31, representing each day of the month. On any given day, you can open the file to the appropriate date, reminding you of invoices that need to be paid and other important items.

The second approach is to maintain a binder,

similar to your chronological file. Write in pencil the date you'll need a particular piece of paper on the upper right-hand corner, three-hole punch it, and place it in the binder (the most recent date in front). Each morning, simply open the binder to determine if there is anything marked with today's date. This is a great way to keep track of sales leads.

Supplies

Each office has unique requirements, which will become self-evident as time passes. Don't rush out and spend a fortune on unnecessary supplies. Start with only the basics and build your inventory in the months ahead. The following list of commonly needed office supplies will serve as a guide:

- Address book or file
- Business card holder
- Correction fluid
- Desk organizer
- Drawer organizer
- Envelopes
- File folders and labels
- Glue
- Hole-punch
- In and out boxes
- Letter opener
- Paper clips
- Pencil holder
- Pencil sharpener
- Postage scale
- Postage stamps
- Rubber bands
- Ruler
- Scissors
- Scotch tape
- Stapler and staples
- Three-ring binders

Stationery

As previously mentioned, stationery is an important part of your overall marketing strategy.

Potential clients are likely to base their first impression of you on correspondence they receive, so make it a positive one. If you cannot afford to buy everything at once, start with business cards first, and then move on to letterhead, brochures, and so on. Ideally, you should hire a professional graphic designer to create a distinctive logo for your company. But be forewarned, this can be expensive. You may be able to employ the services of a friend with artistic experience or a graphic design student.

• Business cards. These are an integral part of everyday business affairs. They are exchanged at both formal and informal meetings and represent an inexpensive and lasting form of advertising. On average, 500 cards cost 25 to 50 dollars. So for about five or 10 cents, you can obtain an almost permanent place in the business card file of a potential customer.

Since they are so affordable, don't settle for the bottom of the line. Get professional-looking card stock and a design that reflects who you are and what your business is about. A business card should include the name of your company, your name, address, and phone number. If you have a logo or slogan, include that as well. If not, you may want to include a list of services provided. Various colors, textures, type styles, graphic designs, and paper weights are available, so explore all the possibilities.

• Letterhead. Your letterhead should be printed

on the same color paper, using the same logo, slogan, type style, and graphic design as your business card. Again, choose quality bond paper to ensure a professional-looking result. If you have a laser printer and want to avoid the expense of letterhead, you can design your own and print it on plain bond paper each time you send out correspondence.

• Brochures, flyers, and invoices. Like letterhead, any brochures, flyers, or invoices sent out from your office should share the same logo, slogan, type style, and graphic design. A consistent, uniform design looks professional and will be memorable. This will help develop an image for your company in the minds of potential customers as they become visually familiar with you.

Procedures Manual

Outline the tasks you perform on a regular basis, listing exactly what is involved with getting each task done. Be as detailed as possible. Write it as if you were explaining it so someone else could take over the assignment. Hopefully, one day you'll be able to delegate some of the easier tasks, and you'll be glad you took the time to write out explanations. Also, write down the format that should be followed for all correspondence out of your office, including letters, invoices, and advertisements.

Create a Brain-Nourishing Environment

"I have no idea what business to start. I have no idea what new products I should offer. I have no idea how to grow my business." Ever hear yourself mutter those sentences? The fact is, to succeed in a home business takes a constant stream of great ideas. Where do they come from? It's not all serendipity. You can actually create a "brain-nourishing" environment that breeds great ideas. Here are some tips to get you started.

• Remember, the factory of the Information Age is the human mind. You don't need employees or expensive equipment to succeed in business today. You do need to tap into both your right brain (creative, divergent thinking) and left brain (analytical, convergent thinking). Set a kitchen clock for 10 minutes and throw out ideas (no matter how outlandish) rapid-fire (right brain activity). Then spend 20 minutes analyzing them (left brain activity).

• The best ideas start with a passion to solve a specific problem or find an answer to a burning question. Simply asking yourself the right questions is a launching pad. The world changed forever when the first nomad stopped asking, "How do we get to water?" and asked instead, "How can we get the water to come to us?"

• If you want to generate great ideas, "Ready, Fire, Aim" should be your motto. Clearly identify the problem by asking the right questions (Ready). Throw out dozens—even hundreds—of possible solutions, from wacky to wonderful, from silly to sublime (Fire). At least one of these ideas is bound to be good, so refine it (Aim). The notebooks of geniuses like Leonardo da Vinci and Albert Einstein are filled with scribbles, doodles, and unconnected thoughts—all evidence of a vigorous Fire stage.

• Newspapers, magazines, and books are filled with idea fodder. So is nature. Children are infinitely creative and can often spark new ideas. When Edwin Land took a picture of his young daughter, she asked, "Why can't we see the picture now?" That question inspired Land to invent the Polaroid Land camera.

• Most ideas come when you're not trying too hard. Many come in the middle of the night. The trick is to write them down immediately so they are not lost. Stock notebooks and microcassette recorders wherever your best ideas usually strike: by your bedside, in the car, and in the bathroom.

• Break mental blocks. If you're bogged down in a problem and need a boost, begin scribbling with a pencil or pick up a small object with your nondominant hand. The unfamiliar muscular movements from the subordinate side of your body will trigger an electrical flow in the nondominant side of your brain. The net result? New connections, a new perspective—possibly a new idea.

• According to research conducted by Chic Thompson, author of *What a Great Idea!* (HarperCollins), the top 10 idea-generating times are when you are:

10. Performing manual labor
9. Listening to a church sermon
8. Waking in the middle of the night
7. Exercising
6. Reading at leisure
5. In a boring meeting
4. Falling asleep or waking up
3. Commuting to work
2. Showering or shaving
1. Sitting on the toilet

• Whether you have a fleeting notion or a product concept you just can't shake, you'll never know whether it's a great idea or a fluke—until you put it out for all the world to see. A fair idea put to use is much better than a great idea kept on the polishing wheel. Remember: It won't fly if you don't try!

Don't re-create the same dull, stark environment that has stifled corporate creativity for years. Replace fluorescent lights with halogen, incandescent, or natural light. Play uplifting classical or jazz music. Sit by the window and daydream! Have a large white board and markers for mapping out projects. Fill your office with flowers, plants, books, stimulating artwork, decorator accents, maybe even a hammock. Make it a place you want to spend time! I love spending time in my home office; my family might say I love it too much! Each morning, after breakfast and morning devotions with the children, I pour myself a tall glass of ice water and head for my home office down the hill. When I report to work, the first thing I do is light some scented candles, then turn on classical music, and I'm ready to generate some great ideas.

Questions

1. Where will you set up your office?

2. List the equipment you will need to get started and ideas for obtaining it.

3. Note your office hours for each day:
   Monday
   Tuesday
   Wednesday
   Thursday
   Friday
   Saturday

(Why not make a large "Mom Working" sign and post it on your office door? Begin holding office hours today!)

4. List the office supplies you will need. Begin to purchase them, one by one if necessary.

Assignments
1. Purchase your supplies and equipment.
2. Set up your filing system.
3. Once you've decided on a company name, have your stationery printed. If you can afford it, hire a professional to design a logo for you or contact a local art school.

CHAPTER NINE

Do You Need a Computer?

Thanks to the increasing affordability of personal computers, many home-based businesswomen ought to consider buying one. However, don't rush out to buy a computer until you've determined that you really do need one and understand what you need it for.

The nature of the work you do is the first criterion to examine. Some jobs lend themselves better to computerization than others. You don't need a computer to crochet baby sweaters, but you can't publish a newsletter without one. In certain professions, a computer is mandatory. Secretaries, writers, salespeople, and anyone else whose business survival demands storing and manipulating information can't survive without the enhancement afforded by a computer.

Also consider the volume of work that could

be computerized. Your home-based crocheting business probably wouldn't require a computer if you are only making three sweaters every month to sell at the local bazaar. But if you are selling hundreds of sweaters via mail, a computer would help maintain a list of customers. That's extremely important because in the mail-order business, your best prospects for future sales are those who have bought from you in the past and know the quality of your products.

Second, you must determine what you need a computer for. If you type only one letter a week, a typewriter would probably suffice. If, on the other hand, you need to keep track of inventory, pay bills, issue invoices, or work with columns of numbers for other reasons, a computer can help. Maintaining a list of previous, existing, or prospective customers will be more simple and efficient with a computer. Today's computers can even help artists, cross-stitchers, fashion designers, architects, and other professionals with software programs designed for creative projects.

Gloria Ghedini of Ghedini Group Tours has found that using a computer has revolutionized her travel service. "It used to take me hours of phone calls to obtain flight schedules, and often the information was wrong anyway," she says. Today, using her computer to access the Internet, Gloria can get immediate, up-to-the-minute details on flight times and rates, car rentals, hotels, and more.

Before You Buy

Before you spend thousands of dollars, think through your purchase carefully and research which computer system is best for you. Once you've determined that you really do need a computer, you must decide where to buy. Ask yourself the following questions:

• Is the vendor reputable? Be sure the store or individual who sells you the hardware and software is willing to back it up. Have they been in business long? Does it seem like they'll be in business for a long time to come? Talk to people who have dealt with the vendor. Are they happy with the equipment and service? Beware of outfits that look fly-by-night even if they offer a seemingly better deal than a more reputable dealer.

• Is one-stop shopping available? Unless you (or someone you trust) are a computer expert, you're probably better off dealing with a store that offers a wide variety of hardware and software. A representative will help you put together a complete package, including computer, printer, software, and accessories. Some computer stores carry only one line of computers. Unbiased advice is more common at diversified stores.

• What support services are available? When it comes to service, be sure to ask questions and get the answers in writing. Find out in advance if the store backs up the products they sell. If you get home and can't figure out how to set things up, can you call for help or are you on your own the minute you walk out the door? If the printer breaks down three months from now, what do you do? What if it breaks down three years from now?

More than likely, the salesman will try to sell you a service contract (which picks up where the warranty leaves off) along with your hardware. Take it home and think it over. If computer equipment is the foundation of your business and neither you nor anyone you know is proficient with computers, a service contract may not be a bad idea. But shop around. If a nearby computer repair shop offers reasonable prices, you can use their service when needed without paying an annual fee. In fact, the price of computer hardware is dropping so rapidly that replacement is often cheaper than repair.

• Is tutorial software included? If you have no prior experience with a particular software program, be sure the package includes a tutorial program (a computerized tutor that will instruct you at your own pace). Of course, you'll be anxious to dive right in when you bring home the "baby," but you'll be spared much frustration if you take the time to work through the tutorial at least once before attempting the real thing.

Hardware

Hardware is the backbone of any computer system. This includes the disc drive, monitor, keyboard, and printer. The most important factor to look for is expandability. Will the system grow with you? Will you be able to upgrade as new technologies become available?

Personal computers have revolutionized American society, and they can do the same for your business. But be sure to think through carefully what features you require before you spend a lot of money for a system too advanced for your needs.

Software

While hardware constitutes the backbone of a computer system, it's the software that "fleshes it out." The software you install on your computer is what makes it uniquely suited to your needs; it's the personal side of the personal computer. A wide array of software programs exists, ranging from daily planners to complete accounting systems. Walking into a software store can make you feel like a kid in a candy shop. But the wise woman will restrict her purchases to those packages she truly needs.

Word Processors

You'll almost certainly need a good word processing package. Whether you're planning to be a free-lance writer or just compose letters to potential customers, life will be much easier without having to fuss over a typewriter. Word processors allow you to change a document an unlimited number of times. As a result, you'll be inclined to let ideas flow more freely, knowing you can always go back and change them later.

Word processors also make it possible to print multiple copies of the same document, so you don't have to retype a standard letter over and over. It also means you can send out customized, high-quality documents rather than impersonal photocopies. This is accomplished through the "merge" feature. That is, you compose your letter, type the names and addresses of everyone you want to send it to, then press a few buttons. The computer will merge the names and addresses into the proper place in your letter, creating individual, personalized copies for each of your clients or customers. Before you know it, you'll have dozens, hundreds, even thousands of customized letters completed.

Most word processors come equipped with an internal dictionary. Press a button, and the computer checks for spelling errors. When it finds a possible error, it will point it out to you (each program does so in a different manner) and offer several ways to correct it. If your spelling is poor, by all means invest in a spell-checker or buy a word processor that includes one.

Another product on the market is the grammar-checker, usually sold separately. If your grammar is worse than your spelling, and you can afford it, you might buy one of these as well.

Be sure to purchase a word processing package that is widely used, particularly in your target industry. WordPerfect and Microsoft Word are widely used in most corporate environments, while WordStar is popular in academic circles. No matter what a "deal" it seems like, resist the temptation to buy an unknown software package just because the price is right.

Database Management Systems

Database management systems do exactly what the name implies—they enable you to manage data. They are most useful for maintaining large mailing lists or product information. Your database will enable you to retrieve detailed information with the touch of a few buttons.

Let's assume you input the name, address, and item purchased for every customer, as well as a note about how they heard of your business. You can then ask the computer to show you all your customers by last name in alphabetical order, or those who live in Detroit, or everyone who purchased Product A, or everyone who heard of your business through a certain newspaper ad. This information will help you make decisions about where to advertise and what type of people to target.

Financial Applications

There are many software programs that can help you manage the financial side of your business. If you want to add columns and rows of numbers, you'll need a spreadsheet, which looks just like a columnar pad, except that the computer does the math for you. Spreadsheets are available in many configurations and applications.

Lotus 1-2-3 and QuattroPro are two of the most popular spreadsheets.

If you want a program to help you manage your business and personal finances, or if you plan to start a bookkeeping service, you can buy personal finance software. Some of the more popular brands include Quicken, MoneyCounts, Managing Your Money, and Dollars & Sense. If you are looking for very affordable software, one place to try is Parsons Technology (1-800-779-6000). Founded as a home-based business by Bob and Martha Parsons, this company now offers a wide variety of excellent programs, most ranging in price from $29 to $49.

Assignment

1. List all your business tasks that lend themselves to computerization. (Note: Take this list with you to the computer shop. It will help determine which hardware and software packages you should buy.)

CHAPTER TEN

The Wonderful World Online

No doubt you've heard all the talk about the Internet, and you're wondering, *Do I need to get online?* The answer, in many cases, is yes. At the time of this writing (1999), approximately 100 million people have Internet host computers. That means only 12 percent of households have a modem-equipped computer, so the growth potential is astronomical. Within the next few years, it's expected that consumers will spend $50 billion online each year. In fact, America's CEOs believe 40 percent of their sales will come through the Internet by 2005. Lest you think the Internet is only for the big guys, think again: 40 percent of small businesses are expected to use the Web to conduct business by the year 2000. Clearly, it's time to get on board!

The Internet, also called cyberspace, is an

international network of computer systems. It began as a communications medium for government and educational institutions. The idea was to share research and information in a format that would offer instant computerized access to anyone, anywhere in the world, anytime of day. Soon, businesses and individuals began tapping into this vast electronic storehouse of information.

A History Lesson

I think my experience typifies the emergence and evolution of the Internet, so let me share some of my journey, as a crash course on the history of cyberspace. When I first began surfing through cyberspace in the early 1990s, my only objective, like most people's, was research—reading articles, reports, and extracts online. The information I accessed was strictly text—no flashy graphics, no point-and-click, no advertisers trying to sell me anything.

Next, I discovered that one of my clients, a graphic designer on the East Coast, had an Internet account. Since I had relocated from the East Coast to Arizona, we realized we could save money by communicating via e-mail instead of the phone. I'll never forget the day I came up with the brilliant idea of trying to send him copy (I wrote company brochures, and he added graphics, then sent it to the printer) over the Internet. We spent all day trying to figure out how to do it! But figure it out we did, and that was the end of the Federal Express bills.

Before long, I was communicating with most of my clients online. I noticed that the Internet was becoming increasingly commercial—that is, more and more businesses were trying to use it as a marketing tool. The emphasis in the mid-1990s was "establishing a presence" on the Internet— few corporations had immediate hopes of generating much income, but at least consumers could look up additional information about their products online.

Do you remember the first time you were watching a TV commercial, and you noticed "www.whatevercompany.com" flashing on the screen? Didn't you wonder what on earth it meant? Pretty soon, most TV commercials were flashing "www." Then "www" started turning up in magazines and newspapers, too.

During the second half of the 1990s, enough people figured out what that "www" stuff was all about and began visiting sites online—to satisfy their curiosity or find out additional information about the company or product being marketed. The Internet was undergoing a transformation, as the number of business sites gradually overshadowed the government, academic, and research-oriented sites. Still, few people had the courage to actually place an order online. Are you kidding? That just seemed crazy!

In early 1996, I received a phone call from Lisa Thomas, formerly an editor with *Home Office Computing* magazine. Lisa and I had worked together on a number of projects, and she was excited to tell me all about her new job with iVillage, "an online content provider and marketing studio." I remember thinking, *What on earth is an online content provider and marketing studio—and what on earth do they want with me?*

I soon found out. As it happens, iVillage pioneered the transformation of the Internet into a full-fledged marketing venue. And I was privileged to be part of it. My job was to serve as the resident SYSOP (system operator) or expert on working from home. I was commissioned to create a "content-oriented" site from scratch. This was pioneering work. In the beginning, I had no idea where the path was leading, but I pressed on and figured it out as I went along. It was exciting and nerve-wracking at the same time. Daily, I wondered, *If I build it, will they come?* We didn't know for sure, but we had hope. We began building.

My first order of business was to develop content for the site. That meant writing articles about working from home, which I e-mailed to the "techies" who transformed my content into the point-and-click format. Once we had enough content to launch the site, called AboutWork, iVillage sent out electronic invitations to potential visitors. (Other experts had been working simultaneously to develop content on various aspects of career and work.) We had built it . . . and slowly, they began coming.

Next, I developed more interactive content: self-tests, quizzes, that sort of thing. In this way, visitors to our site could actually interact with the information, not just read it. We took it to the next level—we opened up message boards, where people could post (or type in) a question. Throughout the day, I would check the message boards and type in my answers. This interaction was quick, but it wasn't instant. Instant was the next step: I began hosting a "chat" once a week. A chat involves meeting in an online conference room where people can talk to one another live. The conversation moves as quickly as people can type. The latest thing (which will soon be old news, I'm sure) is software that enables you to simply talk in the chat room—the computer instantly transcribes your voice into text.

Then one day, the most bizarre thing happened! I logged on to the Internet, reported to work at the site, and there on the corner of the screen was a one-inch by three-inch brown box with the UPS emblem. I scratched my head and thought, *That's odd*. The next day, the box was still there. Hmmm. I clicked the box and was transported to www.ups.com—the UPS Web site. I asked my boss what was up.

"They are our first advertiser," she announced with glee.

"Advertiser? Who would want to advertise on the Internet?" I wondered aloud. "Who's gonna bother to click on an advertisement?" It sounded like a dumb idea to me.

Today, the "little brown box" is called a banner, and the Internet is awash with them. And my naive question has been answered with a vengeance. Who would advertise on the Internet? Every company with enough sense to seize the opportunity. Who would bother to click on an advertisement? Everyone who wants to enjoy the convenience of shopping online.

Getting Started

By the time you read this history lesson, it will probably be ancient history. I can't even imagine what's next for cyberspace. That's why I'm almost reluctant to offer advice . . . but I'll give it a shot. As of this moment, if you want to cash in on the Internet, here's how to get started:

1. Do some basic homework. Surf the Net and check out what the competition is doing. If you'd like to generate income on the net, read *Making Money in Cyberspace: The Inside Information You Need to Start or Take Your Own Business Online* by Paul Edwards, Sarah Edwards, and Linda Rohrbough. You can purchase it at their Web store: www.4expertise.com. You should also check out *The Internet Business Guide* by Rosalind Resnick, *World Wide Web Marketing* by Jim Sterne, and *Guerilla Marketing Online* by Jay Conrad Levinson.

You can purchase Web page creation software programs that will put you on the Web with no programming knowledge necessary. Check out HotDog Professional, Egor Animator, Web Commander, and Submit This! software. (These are widely available at office supply stores, or you can download Web creation software from the Internet.) The most expensive option is hiring a professional Web site creator to do the job for you. Your best bet is probably to design your own homespun page. Then if you get results—or at least sense some serious potential—you can upgrade or invest in a more professional site.

2. Do more than sell at your site. Do you want to walk into a store and get hit over the head with a sales pitch? I doubt it. Yet that's what too many Web sites are like. Instead, offer valuable information, including FAQs (answers to Frequently Asked Questions) related to your industry. Your site should be as educational and entertaining as possible, with plenty of quizzes, self-tests, games, and contests. Provide interactive opportunities, so people will stick around longer, which increases the likelihood that they'll eventually buy.

3. Link up. Include plenty of hyperlinks to "hot sites" related to your products or services. In this way, your site becomes a "launch pad" users will revisit whenever they want information in your industry. Warning: Some sites are little more than links to sites that offer nothing but links to other sites. As a result, the Web searcher never gets any real value. That's a frustrating game you don't want to be part of. Provide solid content so others

will want to provide links to your site as well.

4. Get listed in search engines and directories. To your potential customer, finding your site is like finding a particular store in the Mall of America . . . blindfolded. Make it easy by getting your site listed in Yahoo!, Webcrawler, Lycos, and the hundreds of other directories springing up daily. Services like Postmaster will help you get listed in the right locations (www.netcreations.com/post-master).

5. Publish your Web address on all of your printed material—brochures, business cards, flyers, and so on. Also, create an "electronic signature," including your Web address, and include it on every e-mail and post.

6. Keep current. Frequently update your site with fresh information and "happenings." What constitutes a successful Web site is constantly changing content, and the expectations keep getting higher—today, the best sites change content every hour. Watch the competition and stay informed of trends.

CHAPTER ELEVEN

Legal Issues

Many potential home-based entrepreneurs are scared off by legal hurdles and red tape. I won't sugarcoat things by telling you that legalities and paperwork are not a hassle. However, the amount of red tape will be determined by the size, complexity, and nature of your business. In fact, most home businesses require very little paperwork.

On the other hand, if you are starting big and will be hiring employees, you should seek the advice of a professional lawyer who specializes in small businesses. You will need to ensure compliance with the Fair Labor Standards Act, the Consumer Product Safety Act, and the Occupational Safety and Health Act, just to name a few. The Small Business Administration (SBA) or trade associations related to your industry can also answer any questions you have.

Choosing a Legal Structure

The first legal decision you will have to make is what type of structure your business will assume. Each of the four options are discussed in this section.

• Sole proprietorship. This offers substantial benefits for the home-based businesswoman, and in the vast majority of instances this structure should be chosen. You will not incur any legal fees, because there are no forms to file. You simply register with the city or county clerk, as discussed below, a task you can certainly do without legal assistance. It's important to consider that sole proprietors are permitted to employ their spouses and children without paying Social Security or Federal Unemployment Taxes. That is not the case for a corporation. Chances are, your family will end up on the payroll at some point, so this is an important benefit.

Another factor to consider, which is both an advantage and a disadvantage, is that a sole proprietorship can close its doors at any time. That's good if you have truly given your home business your best shot and things just haven't worked out—or if you've earned so much money that you can retire early. It's not so good, however, when you are tempted to throw in the towel without allowing enough time for your business to develop.

Under a sole proprietorship, all profits and losses are attributed to you personally. So if your business will involve taking major financial risks, you should seriously consider adopting a corporate structure. Otherwise, you will just need to file a Schedule C, "Profit or Loss from Business or Profession, " when you file your 1040 Form at the end of the year. If you earn more than $400 you will also have to file a Schedule SE, "Social Security Self-Employment Tax." You can obtain a copy of the Small Business Administra-tion's Form 2065, which is an application for a sole proprietorship, either online (www.sba.gov) or from your local SBA office.

• Partnership. The tax ramifications of a partnership are very similar to a sole proprietorship, except that partners split the income or loss reported on their respective 1040 Forms at the end of each year. Many states have a Uniform Partnership Act that defines a partnership as "an association of two or more persons to carry on as co-owners of a business for profit."[1]

A partnership can be based on a verbal agreement, but a written document is a wise precaution. Some of the things you should spell out in a written partnership agreement include:

1. Allocation of profits and losses (e.g., 50-50, 60-40)
2. Salary provisions
3. Capital to be invested by each party
4. Provisions for the death or disability of one of the partners
5. Terms relating to the termination of the partnership

• Corporation. A legal corporation is by far the most complex structure your home-based business can assume. If you are planning to hire a large number of employees, then you will have to incorporate your business. Some other factors to consider include better pension and profit-sharing options for your employees; group insurance rates (the premiums for which are fully deductible for the first $50,000 of coverage); and medical benefits, also fully deductible. In addition, there are capital gains tax benefits available to corporations, which are not available to individuals or partnerships. The first step in this process is to hire a lawyer or accountant.

• Sub S Corporation. The Sub S Corporate structure can be used if your business will show a loss. By applying for Sub S status, you can obtain certain tax benefits. Be sure to consult a tax expert if you think you may qualify.

For more information on legal structure, check out the Small Business Administration Web site at www.sba.gov.

Choosing and Registering a Name

If you elect to operate as a sole proprietor, you are permitted by law to operate under your own name. However, if presenting a professional image is important to you, then it is advisable to choose an official name for your business. Also, keep in mind that banks will not allow you to open a business account until you have a registration certificate in hand.

When choosing a name, be sure it can grow with you. The name Apples-R-Us may seem cute now, but what if you start selling oranges? On the other hand, if you are a toy maker and won't be expanding into other areas, a name that clearly identifies what you do is best. Contact your county clerk's office to learn the procedures for obtaining a "doing business as" or trade name.

Post Office Box

When you register your trade name, you will be asked to provide a business address. Keep in mind that this address will become public knowledge and within several days, you can expect to receive a truckload of mail from people who want to sell you products and services. It may be advisable to open a post office box in your company's name to prevent the dissemination of your home address.

Sales Tax

Most state governments (and many municipalities) levy a sales tax on merchandise. If you sell or resell a product, you will need a sales authorization certificate. This assigns you a resale tax number so you can buy material wholesale and not have to pay sales tax on it until it is resold, either incorporated into your final product or as is.

You must collect sales tax on everything you sell directly to consumers, then remit the money to the appropriate government office. The percentage varies from state to state, so contact your

State Department of Taxation, Sales Tax Bureau, for more details.

Licenses and Permits

Depending on the nature of your business, your state or local government may require you to obtain certain licenses or permits before you begin operation. For example, a hairstylist requires a license, and day-care facilities may need special permits. If you are unsure of the requirements for your particular line of business, contact the Small Business Administration or your trade association.

Zoning Regulations

Most states, counties, and municipalities have zoning restrictions on the types of businesses that may be conducted in certain areas. You may not be permitted to board horses or open a beauty salon in your housing complex. There is usually a zoning office at county headquarters or city hall. You may also be able to contact your State Office of Economic Development to obtain material outlining restrictions on home-based businesses on a state level. Again, if in doubt, contact your local Small Business Administration office.

Insurance

Be sure to contact your insurance agent to discuss necessary changes to your policy. This is particularly important if you plan to invest in office equipment or will need to maintain inventory in your home. Some of the issues you should discuss include:

1. Fire, theft, and casualty damage to equipment and inventory
2. Liability coverage for customers, vendors, or others who may visit your home business
3. Product liability coverage if you make or sell a product
4. Professional liability if you will be offering a service
5. Additional car insurance if you will be using your family vehicle for business purposes

Your insurance agent will almost certainly require a copy of your business plan (see chapter 6). Also, be sure to ask if you are entitled to a discount on your homeowner's policy, since working at home much of the time reduces the chance of fire and burglary.

Questions

1. Which legal structure will you assume?

2. List 10 possible names for your business. Now begin to narrow it down until you find the right one. (Warning: This might take a lot longer than you think. Be sure to get opinions from family and friends as well.)

Assignments

1. Check on zoning laws, if warranted.
2. Open a post office box, if desired.
3. Register your name with the city or county clerk.
4. Apply for applicable licenses or permits.
5. Talk to your insurance agent.

CHAPTER TWELVE

Finances

L ike legal issues, business finances may be unknown territory for the new home-based businesswoman. However, once the terms are understood and a few points clarified, finances become far less daunting. Hopefully, this brief overview will familiarize you with some commonly used financial terms and practices.

Deductible Expenses

When it comes to taxes, you are expected to pay your fair share. Paying more is foolish. As a self-employed businesswoman, you are entitled to certain deductions; don't be afraid to make use of them.

• Your home. If you use part of your home exclusively or regularly for business, and it serves as your principal place of business, you are entitled to deduct costs as a business expense.

Exclusively means that portion of your home that is used for business and nothing else. You cannot deduct your bedroom or kitchen if you use part of it for business and part of it for family. The deduction is allowable only if you have an entire room set aside for business. The one exception is inventory storage. For example, if you use half of the basement to store products, you can deduct it. You may also deduct for other facilities located on your property, such as a greenhouse, artist's studio, or garage, if they are used solely for business purposes. *Regularly* means that even though you don't devote your full time to conducting your business at home, you do so on a regular basis. Your home is your principal place of business if you spend more than 50 percent of the time devoted to a particular job at home (in other words, your home can qualify even if your business is a side job).

The deduction allowed is based on the percentage of your house used. The most acceptable way to determine this is to calculate the square footage of your office as a percentage of the entire square footage of your house. Or you can approximate using the following method: Let's assume you have a three-bedroom house with a dining room, kitchen, and living room, and all six rooms are approximately the same size. If one of the rooms serves as your office, you can deduct one-sixth of the mortgage, real estate tax, electricity, homeowners insurance, and so on, as a business expense.

• Indirect expenses. Even putting on a new roof, painting the exterior, and other such renovations and repairs are all considered indirect expenses related to your business and are partially deductible based on the percentage.

• Direct expenses. Directly related expenses, such as painting or carpeting the office, are fully deductible. However, keep in mind that the total deduction taken for the business use of your home cannot exceed the gross income earned from the business. To simplify your expense recording throughout the year, incorporate the preprinted expense forms (chapter 20) into your personal notebook.

• Travel. Whenever you take a trip for the sole purpose of conducting or promoting your business, all expenses—airfare, car rental, lodging, meals—are fully deductible.

• Entertainment and business gifts. You can also deduct the cost of lunches, dinners, tickets, etc., incurred while cultivating clients or prospects. A five-minute discussion with your best friend about how things are going does not constitute a business lunch. The event must be directly related to the active conduct of your business.

• Education and training. If you attend seminars, classes, or conventions to further your business skills, you can deduct fees, tuition, and books, as well as transportation and incidental expenses.

• Local transportation. When you run general business errands—to the store or a client's site, for example—you are entitled to deduct mileage, parking, and tolls. Or you can deduct a percentage of gas, oil, tires, insurance, repairs, or even the cost of a new car. (To determine the correct percentage, keep track of how many miles are used exclusively for business and how many miles were traveled overall throughout the year.) Please note that you cannot have it both ways. You may use either the per mile deduction or the percentage method.

• Research events. Any time you take a trip to acquire information necessary for your business, whether it's to the local library or to check out the competition, the expenses you incur are deductible (mileage, parking, library materials, etc.).

• Donations. If you donate one of your products to charity, such as a handcrafted vase, the actual worth (not the sale price) of the item is deductible.

• Regular expenses. Any expenses you incur in the regular course of business are fully deductible, including installation of a telephone (or a percentage of your telephone bill, plus actual business calls), an answering machine, computer or any other equipment. But don't forget the little things, which can add up (tape, envelopes, postage, paper clips, pens, stationery). Advertising expenses, business cards, and interest payments on loans are also deductible. Whenever possible, pay for business expenses by check and obtain receipts. Taking an extra minute to write an explanation on the back of the receipt will be a tremendous help when tax season rolls around.

When to Pay Taxes

By the time you file your tax return, you should have paid 80 percent of total income tax and Social Security tax due for the year. This is accomplished by filing Form 1040-ES, "Declaration of Estimated Tax," and paying the estimated tax based on how much you have earned over the preceding three months. The deadlines for quarterly filings are January 15, April 15, June 15, and September 15. Your state government may also require quarterly filings.

Employees

If you employ anyone, you are required to obtain Form SS-4 to receive an Employer's Identification Number. You will pay 6.7 percent of the employee's earnings to Social Security and deduct 6.7 percent from the employee's paycheck as well.

Federal Tax Identification Number

You must obtain a Federal Tax Identification Number if you have even one employee at any given point. Once obtained, the IRS will send quarterly and year-end payroll tax returns that must be returned even if you no longer have an employee.

Employee's Withholding Allowance

IRS Form W-4, the employee's withholding allowance, indicates marital status and the number of exemptions to be withheld from each paycheck. This form is filled out by each employee and retained by you as the basis for withholding taxes.

You should contact the Division of Labor Standards, U.S. Department of Labor, for information on minimum wage laws, overtime, discrimination, and a host of other matters.

Subcontractors

If you would rather avoid all this red tape, your best bet is to hire independent contractors—that is, people who will work for you on their own time and declare their earnings directly to the government. You do not deduct taxes and are only required to give a Form 1099 to any independent contractor who earns more than $600 in a given year.

A Word of Warning

Please be aware that tax matters are extremely complex. This section was designed to provide some tips but is by no means intended as a complete guide to taxes. You should consult a tax expert who can help you with your specific questions.

The IRS publication #587 titled "Business Use of Your Home" outlines the income tax regulations specific to a home-based business. The

IRS publication "Tax Guide for Small Business" is also very helpful. You can obtain copies of both at your local IRS office. You can even reach our good friends with the IRS at www.irs.gov, where they provide a wealth (pardon the pun) of information on the tax laws pertaining to home business. You can even download the necessary forms.

You can also check out the Small Business Administration's site at www.sba.gov. It offers a comprehensive listing of their small business programs and publications, along with reports, statistics, and studies related to various fields of endeavor. If you're not online, you can contact the SBA at 1-800-UASKSBA.

Record Keeping

The IRS doesn't specify what record keeping format you must use, but you are required by law to retain permanent, accurate, and complete records that clearly represent your earnings, deductions, and credits. Proper record keeping is an important tool for measuring and enhancing profitability, and it has been proven to increase the likelihood of business success.

According to the Small Business Administration, a good record-keeping system has six primary characteristics:

1. Simple to use
2. Easy to understand
3. Reliable

4. Accurate
5. Consistent
6. Designed to provide information on a timely basis

The components of your system should include a format to track expenses, record income, and compare the two. You can purchase a complete record-keeping system, including instructions for its use, at any stationery store. You can also hire an accountant to set up a customized system for you. You may find the forms provided in this book helpful as well. In any case, be sure to include the following:

Cash Disbursements Journal

All expenditures for your business should be recorded in a cash disbursements journal. Don't wait until you have a purse full of receipts before you try to organize them; discipline yourself to record expenses as they are incurred. Your notebook should have a section for "Expenses," along with an envelope for receipts. You can then transfer the information into your detailed journal, which breaks down expenses by category. It should look something like this:

Date	Total $	Description	Supplies	Postage	Advertising
8-5-99	16.22	File Folders	16.22		
8-7-99	50.00	Stamps		50.00	

The categories you need will depend upon your unique business, but they will likely include transportation, entertainment, telephone, utilities, stationery, and consulting fees. At the end of each month, total each category. This will give you an excellent idea of where your money is going.

Tracking expenses is easier if you pay for most items using your business checking account. A petty cash fund is also helpful for those occasions when check writing isn't warranted (items under $5). You can make up your own petty cash forms or purchase preprinted ones at a stationery store, and use them when a receipt isn't available for small purchases.

Sales Journal

Depending upon the nature of your business, your sales journal may reflect cash register totals on a daily basis or invoices awaiting payment. The first is termed "cash basis" bookkeeping; the latter is called "accrual basis." Cash-based records are straightforward: Carefully record each day's sales totals in a journal.

But if you will be invoicing clients (accrual basis), you should set up a system along the following lines:

Date	Date Rec'd	Customer	Invoice Amount	Product A	B	Sales Tax	Shipping
7-1-99	7-20-99	Stan's Flower	$34.87	10.00/24.87		$1.67	$2.45
7-2-99	8-3-99	Gifts & Such	$56.88	22.41/34.47		$2.89	$4.78

As you total this information each month, you will learn not only the dollar value of sales but also which products are selling and which are not, so you can adjust your inventory accordingly. You can also see at a glance which customers haven't paid and which customers consistently pay late. You will also know how much sales tax you need to remit to the state. If your shipping expenses are significant, perhaps you can negotiate a volume discount rate with a freight company.

Once you know both your income and expenses, all that remains is to compare the two. Hopefully, income will come out on top every month!

Record Retention

Records that should be kept permanently include cash books, general ledgers, journals, financial statements, audit reports and income tax returns. For six to seven years, you should keep accounts payable and receivable records, canceled checks, inventory records, payroll records, sales receipts, and invoices. Records pertaining to payroll taxes should be kept four years.

Budgeting

You will need to develop two types of budgets for your home-based business: start-up and operating. Worksheets for both can be found at the end of this chapter.

Start-Up Costs

The start-up budget is exactly what it sounds like. It represents your best estimates of how much

money will be required to get your business under-
way and includes equipment purchases, phone
installation, major office supplies, and whatever
else you will need to begin. Many of these will be
one-time expenses. Once you've determined how
much you will need, the next step is to draw upon
your savings account, turn to relatives, or if necessary, visit your local bank to discuss a loan.

Operating Budget

This budget projects income and expenses on
a month-by-month basis for the first year of operation. Some of the categories you will need to
budget for include telephone, office supplies,
postage, transportation, entertainment, advertising, professional service fees (accounting and
legal), insurance, utilities, taxes, and depreciation.

This, of course, is rather difficult to do and you
may want to seek the advice of an accountant. The
Small Business Administration's Service Corps of
Retired Executives (SCORE) staff may also be
able to help.

Most experts recommend that you have the
equivalent of three to six months' expenditures in
reserve, in case your income estimates do not
materialize as planned. Do take that into consideration if you are applying for a loan.

Budget Versus Actual

Once you begin operations, each month you
should compare how much income you actually

earned and how much expenditures you actually incurred with the amounts budgeted for each. If you realize that your budget is unrealistic, you will need to make adjustments accordingly.

Planning is the key to good budgeting, and good budgeting is the key to profitability. Decide not only what you can spend (and no more) but what you will spend (and no less). One of the hardest things for many people to accept is the reality that they have to spend money to make money. That means taking risks, which is hard. So decide in advance how much you are willing to risk to make your business succeed, and then stick to it.

Banking

The key to successful banking is building a relationship with your local banker. Since you have a small business (at least for now), it's best to choose a small, neighborhood bank. As the saying goes, better to be a big fish in a small pond than a small fish in a big pond. Make it a point to get to know the local manager.

Checking Accounts

One of the first things you must do is open a checking account. Having a separate business checking account is an excellent way to ensure that good records are kept, because deposits represent your income, and checks or other withdrawals represent your expenses. If you will be conducting business under any name other than your own, be sure to bring your trade-name certificate and several forms of identification.

Before opening a checking account, you should consider some of the following:

1. Is there a minimum deposit required to open the account?
2. What is the waiting period for fund availability on local and out-of-state checks?
3. What are the stop-payment fees?
4. What is the fee for bounced checks?
5. Is there a transaction fee on checks or deposits?
6. Does the bank offer overdraft protection?
7. What service fees, if any, are charged?

Most banks offer discount loan rates to preferred customers, usually meaning anyone who maintains a checking or savings account with the bank. Keep that in mind when deciding where to open your checking account.

Once you have opened your business checking account, treat it with at least as much care as you would your family account. When your monthly statement arrives, reconcile it with your checkbook immediately. If there are any discrepancies, contact your bank. Store canceled checks in an orderly fashion. Keep blank checks in a safe place; they are almost as good as cash to a thief.

Savings Accounts

If you are a sole proprietor of a small business and will not be writing many checks, you may open a business savings account only. Any checks you do write would be from your personal account. This enables you to avoid paying checking service charges, which can be quite high. In return for some inconvenience, you will even receive interest on your deposits. Check with your accountant to see if this arrangement is best for you.

Automatic Teller Machines

Automatic teller machines (ATMs) make banking convenient. They can be used any time, day or night. Best of all, they are springing up all over—in malls, fast-food restaurants, anywhere you might need emergency cash. Find out if your bank charges a transaction fee for deposits and withdrawals from ATMs, and if so, how much. These can add up over time.

You will also want to find out which ATM network the bank belongs to and be sure there are locations close to your home. If you travel a great deal, make sure the ATM network has locations in the cities or states you frequently visit.

Loans

Banks are in the business of lending money, and they want to lend to you. All they need is a few good reasons to do so. You can greatly improve your chances of obtaining a loan simply by keeping in mind the following tips:

• Choose a local bank. In most instances, a small, community-oriented bank will be much more willing to work with you than a gigantic, city-based financial institution. Don't apologize for operating a small business and don't plead as if the bank is doing you a personal favor. Rest assured that they intend to make a good profit from your loan, however much or little you borrow.

• Demonstrate your credibility. The loan officer sitting behind that desk wants to lend you money; that's how he makes his living. But he needs assurance that you will be able to repay the loan. Your job is to convince him that your business is viable. Provide him with a copy of your business plan. Show him samples or photographs of your products, or provide a copy of a brochure describing your services.

The loan officer wants to talk dollars and cents, so bring your accountant with you. If you don't have one, bring along whoever will be handling the books. If that's you, make sure to brush up on your accounting procedures so you don't look like a novice.

• Be prepared to put up collateral. In other words, if you are unable to repay the loan from your business earnings, you can cash in these items to cover your debt. This is assurance for the bank that they will get their money back, even if your business fails. Savings accounts, stocks and bonds, and your home mortgage are all examples of collateral.

• Allow enough time. Generally speaking, you should allow at least three months from the time you walk into the bank until you actually have the money in hand. And be sure to apply for more money than you think you need, since the bank is almost certain to offer you less than what you apply for.

Having said all that about the how-tos of borrowing money from a bank, I would strongly discourage you from doing so. Far better to borrow the money from a friend or relative. Better still to let the business be self-funding. That is, invest your own time and energy, rather than someone else's money.

Is It a Home Business or Hobby?

How does the IRS decide whether you have a legitimate home business or are just trying to write off expenses related to a hobby? Simply put, you must show that you intend to make a profit. As a rule of thumb, the IRS says your business should show a profit three of five consecutive years. However, even if you don't make a profit three out of five years, you can still demonstrate that your business is legitimate if you:

• Carry on your activities in a business-like fashion, keeping financial records and following normal business procedures.

• Demonstrate that you have (or are developing) expertise in your field.

• Keep careful records of time invested.

This distinction is extremely important. If your activity is a hobby, you can deduct expenses related to the activity as an itemized deduction subject to the 2 percent of adjusted gross income limitation, but you cannot deduct more than the income from your hobby. However, if your activity is a business, you can deduct all of your expenses. If your expenses exceed your business income, you can deduct the excess from other income. And that will make a big difference in your total tax liability.

Business Use of the Home[1]

To qualify to claim expenses for the business use of your home, you must meet the following tests.

1. Your use must be:
    a. Exclusive (however, see Exceptions to Exclusive Use)
    b. Regular
    c. For your trade or business, and
2. The business part of your home must be one of the following:
    a. Your principal place of business for your trade or business, or
    b. A place of business where you meet or deal with patients, clients, or customers in the normal course of your trade or business, or
    c. A separate structure (not attached to your home) that you use in connection with your trade or business.

Exclusive Use

To qualify under the exclusive use test, you must use a specific area of your home only for your trade or business. The area used for business can be a room or other space identified as separate. The space does not need to be marked off by a permanent partition. You do not meet the requirements of the exclusive use test if you use the area in question both for business and for personal purposes.

Exceptions to Exclusive Use

You do not have to meet the exclusive use test if:

1. You use part of your home for the storage of inventory or product samples (discussed next), or

2. You use part of your home as a day-care facility, discussed later under Day-Care Facility.

Storage of Inventory or Product Samples

When you use part of your home for the storage of inventory or product samples, the exclusive use test does not apply. However, you must meet all the following five tests.

1. You keep the inventory or product samples for use in your trade or business.

2. Your trade or business is the wholesale or retail selling of products.

3. Your home is the only fixed location of your trade or business.

4. You use the storage space on a regular basis.
5. The space you use is identifiably separate space suitable for storage.

Regular Use

To qualify under the regular use test, you must use a specific area of your home for business on a continuing basis. You do not meet the test if your business use of the area is only occasional or incidental, even if you do not use that area for any other purpose.

Place to Meet Patients, Clients, or Customers

If you meet or deal with patients, clients, or customers in your home in the normal course of your business, even though you also carry on business at another location, you can deduct your expenses for the part of your home used exclusively and regularly for business if:

- You physically meet with patients, clients, or customers on your premises, and
- Their use of your home is substantial and integral to the conduct of your business.

Assignments

1. Obtain any necessary government forms.
2. Open a business bank account.
3. Apply for loan, if warranted.
4. Complete the projected budget forms on the following pages.

Start-Up Budget

I. Sources of Funds

  1. Sources: Amount

    _____   _____

    _____   _____

    _____   _____

II. Uses of Funds

  1. Capital Equipment: Estimated Cost

    _____   _____

    _____   _____

    _____   _____

  2. Office Supplies:

    _____   _____

    _____   _____

    _____   _____

  3. Work Material:

    _____   _____

    _____   _____

    _____   _____

  4. Printed Matter/Advertising:

    _____   _____

    _____   _____

    _____   _____

  5. Other:

    _____   _____

    _____   _____

First-Year Operating Budget

(Note: You will need to extend this budget out to 12 months using a columnar pad or large piece of paper.)

	January	
	Budget	Actual
1. Cash On Hand (Start of month)	_____	_____
2. Cash Received		
Income	_____	_____
Loan	_____	_____
3. Total Cash Available (Total 1 & 2)	_____	_____
4. Disbursements		
a. Office Supplies	_____	_____
b. Postage	_____	_____
c. Telephone	_____	_____
d. Car, Travel	_____	_____
e. Entertainment	_____	_____
f. Advertising/Promotion	_____	_____
g. Accounting, Legal Fees	_____	_____
h. Insurance	_____	_____
i. Utilities	_____	_____
j. Taxes and Depreciation	_____	_____
k. Interest	_____	_____
l. Loan Payment	_____	_____
m. Payroll	_____	_____

n. Other (specify):   ＿＿＿＿＿   ＿＿＿＿＿
                             ＿＿＿＿＿   ＿＿＿＿＿
                             ＿＿＿＿＿   ＿＿＿＿＿
                             ＿＿＿＿＿   ＿＿＿＿＿
Total Cash Paid Out   ＿＿＿＿＿   ＿＿＿＿＿

5. Cash Position
   (3 minus 4)   ＿＿＿＿＿   ＿＿＿＿＿

Part Three

CONSIDERING THE OPTIONS

FAQs: Frequently Asked Questions About Working from Home

Are people really working from home, or is it just hype?

It's for real! According to LINK Resources, a market research firm, 47 million Americans now work from home on a full- or part-time basis. Of those, 18.4 million are self-employed and 55 percent are male; the average age of homeworkers is 40 years old. It's no longer a fad but a genuine trend. In fact, the number of homeworkers has doubled since 1989.

Who will "hire" me to work from home?

No one. Ads claiming to hire homeworkers invariably try to sell you a directory or some such scam. If a company had a *legitimate* opportunity for homeworkers, would they have to *advertise?* THINK! Their existing workforce would leap at the opportunity, then tell their family and friends, who would leap at the opportunity. It would never make it to the local classifieds, let alone national magazines. Bottom line: If you want to be an employee, get a job. If you want to work from home, start your own business.

How can I avoid getting scammed?

Change your mind-set. You must lose forever the notion that there is some "quick and easy way" to make money at home. There are no short-cuts, so stop looking for one. No one is going to hand you a legitimate home business. If you really want to work from home, you'll have to do it the old-fashioned way: Wrack your brains for ideas, research your market, roll up your sleeves, and get to work.

What are the really "hot" businesses to get into?

Over the past decade, I've answered thousands of questions about working from home. The one question that annoys me is, "What's a hot business to get into?" Generally speaking, that's not a good question to ask. One person's sure-thing is another person's disaster-waiting-to-happen. The right business for you is the one you have the experience, skill, and passion to make succeed. With that caveat in mind, *convenience businesses are hot:*
  • temporary help
  • home health care
  • personal shopping

• children's transportation

Equipping people to succeed is also hot:

• computer training

• business consulting

• success coaching

• seminars

• Internet marketing

Keeping in mind that what's "hot" today won't be "hot" tomorrow, here are my current Top Five Picks:

1. *Information brokerage.* There's more information in one issue of *The New York Times* than the average 18th-century person had to absorb in his or her lifetime. If you have a research background—or enjoy detail work—become an information broker. Surf the Internet ferreting out information (legal, financial, market research) for corporations, institutions, or associations. You'll need a fast modem and working knowledge of the Internet. Information brokering and research is a $13 billion industry.

Start-up costs: $5,000 + for hardware and software.

Income: Charge $50 to $150 per hour; earn $75,000+

Contact: Information Industry Association, 555 New Jersey Ave. NW, Suite 800, Washington, D.C. 20001, or Association of Independent Information Professionals, 3724 FM 1960 West, Suite 214, Houston, TX 77068; (713) 537-9051; www.aiip.org.

2. *Mail order.* This $266 billion industry is easy to enter. You can start slow, perhaps with just one product, and build an empire. Develop a product with a target market in mind. Next, write an informative booklet related to your product. Send press releases to every magazine your prospects read, offering your free booklet in return for a self-addressed stamped envelope. Send the booklet plus a sales pitch and order form to your instant mailing list. If you've targeted your market right—and offer a product that solves their problems—they'll buy.

Start-up costs: $100+

Income: $5,000 to $500,000+

Contact: Direct Marketing Association, 11 West 42nd Street, New York, NY 10036; (212) 768-7277; www.thedma.org

3. *Children's transportation service.* The time gap between when kids get out of school and parents return from work is your business opportunity. Drive kids to and from school, and from school to activities and then home. You'll need a minivan with a colorful sign, a special transportation license, and liability insurance. Post flyers around the school, hand out business cards to parents, network at PTA meetings and school fairs. Hand out free balloons with your company name and phone number. Get some publicity in the local paper. Pretty soon, parents will come to you.

Start-up costs: $3,000+ for license, insurance, miscellaneous red tape, and marketing. (This cost estimate assumes you already have a mini-van; if not, your start-up costs increase greatly.)

Income: $3,000 per month+

Contact: National Children's Transport Association, c/o Crusin' Kids Carpool, 4801 S. University Drive #305E, Davie, Fla. 33328; (954) 252-9115; http://gator.naples.net/clubs/ncta/

4. *Temporary services.* This $35 billion industry is red-hot. Interview, test, and register qualified secretarial applicants. (Actually, any field is ripe for temp workers: lawyers, nurses, cooks, factory workers.) Once you have a dozen good candidates, conduct a phone campaign to local companies. You'll need a first-class brochure and business cards. Network at the Chamber of Commerce and with former colleagues. Send out press releases and sell like crazy. If you can get one large corporation to give you a shot, you're on your way.

Start-up costs: $10,000+

Income: $10,000–$70,000+ (Depends on the industry and how many temps you can place.)

Contact: National Association of Temporary and Staffing Services 119 South Saint Asaph Street, Alexandria, Va., 22314-3119; (703) 549-6287; www.natss.org.

5. *Internet marketing.* Virtually every corporation wants a presence on the Internet, but most lack the expertise to launch their own site. Learn HTML and Java programming languages. Study the most successful Web sites and launch your

own to showcase your expertise and attract customers. (Read *The Internet Business Guide* by Rosalind Resnick and *Web Publisher's Design Guide* by Mary Jo Fahey.) If necessary, do a free Web page for an influential business owner in return for a written endorsement and word-of-mouth marketing opportunities.

Start-up costs: $5,000+ (to launch a class site)
Income: Charge $1,000 to $20,000+ per client
Contact: (No association exists.)

Can I really become a millionaire working from home?

Since I'm not a millionaire, I don't feel qualified to answer this question. So, I'll let my business mentor, Dr. Michael LeBoeuf, answer it for me: "Although statistics report that most Americans are working harder and getting poorer, I'm happy to report that my experience is just the opposite. In 1977, I started a second career with a notepad and a ballpoint pen. I was a professor making about $20,000 a year, hoping to supplement my income by writing a book. With that decision, I began a second career in the business of creating and selling information. In 1991, my net worth reached $1 million, and today's it's closer to $2 million.

"What's most important is *how* I achieved financial freedom. I started with no money, just my wits. I never borrowed a cent. I never took any stressful risks. I didn't quit my day job until I was well on my way to financial independence. I have never hired a single employee or rented office space. I've never had a business plan."[1]

I don't know if I'll ever become a millionaire, but if I do, I'm gonna do it just like Mike! In fact, even if you don't have the least interest in becoming a millionaire, you'd still be wise to follow Dr. LeBoeuf's advice: never borrow money, never take stressful risks, never hire anyone, never rent office space, and by all means, keep your day job.

What's the difference between an "entrepreneur" and a "work-from-homer"?

Entrepreneurs are bold risk takers with grand visions of giant empires. They prepare elaborate business plans, borrow money, rent office space, and hire employees.

Work-from-homers have different goals: putting family first, freedom from the corporate grind, the opportunity to use their talents to create their dream lifestyle. Here's how Dr. LeBoeuf puts it: "We want to make a million from home with no payroll, no debts, no employee headaches, and no sleepless nights!"

Speaking for myself, I have no interest in grand empires, and I certainly don't want employees. Are you kidding? I've been an employee, so I know what a hassle we are! To tell the truth, I'm not particularly interested in making a million (but God, if you want to send it, I'll think of ways to spend it . . . wisely). But I'm definitely interested in contributing to our family finances and doing work I love, while keeping my family first. If those are your goals, working from home is definitely for you.

What do most homeworkers do?

The possibilities are endless. However, the most common businesses are service-based rather than product-based. That's because they require less capital to launch and have lower overhead, hence higher profit margin. Consulting is especially popular. People sell their expertise in starting and managing a business; buying, using, and maintaining computers; and making the most of business and personal finances. Marketing is also big business: from advertising and public relations mini-agencies to graphic design and freelance commercial copywriting. The most explosive growth is in the area of Internet marketing.

Can I really make "$4,000 a month with my home computer"?

That's like asking, "Can I make money with my desk lamp?" The lamp will make you more efficient, but it's only a tool. A computer will boost your productivity, but it cannot create a business. Only a human being can do that. As for companies that advertise such "opportunities," many have been hit with fraud charges by the FTC. The only way to make money at home is by *using your head*.

How much should I hope to earn?

Don't expect to earn any profit for the first six months. It takes at least that long to establish your business, attract a few clients, and cover your start-up costs. According to LINK Resources, the average household income of homeworkers is $54,300. Whether you generate more or less depends on the nature of your business, your credentials, your goals, and your time investment. Some businesses generate $100 a week; others generate $100,000 a year.

CHAPTER FOURTEEN

Information Technologies

University of Southern California Professor Jack Nilles has coined the term "telecommuting" to describe the phenomenon of people "commuting" to work not by cars but by computers. Alvin Toffler, author of *Future Shock* and *The Third Wave,* predicts an increasing trend toward home-based, technology-based industries, which he termed "electronic cottages." Both of these futurists believe the office and factory will largely disappear as the central place of business becomes the home.

Anyone who spends time commuting to work each morning has a good idea just how much time and energy are wasted in idling or slow-moving automobiles. For example, if you commute just 30 minutes each way, you spend 250 hours per year, or the equivalent of six 40-hour work weeks, on the road.

Another motivation behind the telecommuting phenomenon is concern for the environment. Commuting via computer creates significantly less pollution than driving a car to and from the workplace. Another important factor is that America is now largely an information-based economy, and information jobs can be easily transferred to the home. More than 50 percent of all jobs in this country are related to the handling, dissemination, storage, and interpretation of information. Marketing, data processing, bookkeeping, publishing, insurance, and computing are just a few information-based industries that lend themselves well to home-based businesses.

Thanks to the Internet and advanced telecommunications capabilities, sitting in your home office is actually more efficient than sitting in an office downtown. Realizing this, many major corporations are now actively developing programs to allow their employees to work from home.

Hundreds of companies have already implemented telecommuting programs, involving tens of thousands of employees. Many more companies are considering this option. If you are currently employed and think you could perform your duties effectively from home, why not propose serving as a test case for a corporate telecommuting program?

If you have a more entrepreneurial spirit, you can turn your skills into a free-lance business. Having already developed a solid network of contacts during your years in the business world, you are well on your way to home-based business success. The tools of technology have become so affordable that free-lancers are now able to compete with major corporations, both in terms of pricing and workmanship.

Donna Agnello: Taking Advantage of Technology

Donna Agnello always dreamed of having her own business someday. She grew up in a home attached to the Bucks County Tennis Club, owned and operated by her parents, so she knew the advantages of an entrepreneurial lifestyle. But the road back home has been long and winding.

Donna grew bored with college after two years and decided to relocate from her parents' country home to New York City, with the dream of a music career foremost in her mind. Instead, she landed a job with *Glamour* magazine and worked her way up from secretary to assistant editor.

Along the way, she accumulated a wide variety of skills, including typing, writing, editing, and design and layout. She was surprised to discover she had talents in many of these areas and had never realized it. Donna found herself increasingly intrigued with the marketing-oriented aspects of her job and decided to move in that direction.

She landed a job as public relations director for Peddler's Village, a quaint Pennsylvania town filled with antique and specialty shops. There she handled all aspects of marketing and promotion, from developing brochures to planning radio and print advertisements.

Although Donna enjoyed the work, she had never let go of the dream of being her own boss. So she began to explore, with the help of a career counselor, potential avenues to pursue. After a series of tests to evaluate her skills and interests, she decided that operating a word processing service was her best option.

In February 1988, with a supportive husband by her side and a $10,000 loan from her parents, Donna invested in state-of-the-art equipment to begin Editype Concepts. She recouped the investment money within the first year. Nevertheless, her earnings were not enough to meet all expenses, so she continued working two days a week for Peddler's Village.

Actually, this worked out well because Donna was able to continue making business contacts through her work for the Village. As a result, Editype Concepts began to evolve. By combining various aspects of both careers, Donna discovered a more interesting and lucrative line of work.

Eventually, Donna found a useful niche. "I think of myself as a small businessman's ad agency," she says. "They don't have the budget to hire a large agency, and I've got the skills and technology to be their one-stop shop." Since her computer system has desktop publishing capabilities, Donna is able to create newsletters, brochures, and advertisements for her clients. And thanks to her media placement experience, she can then help clients use the documents she creates in promotional campaigns.

There is, however, a down side to Donna's business. "If there is one thing that I absolutely detest, it's having to drum up business," she says. "I enjoy doing the work; it's finding it that I hate." Which is why she has focused her attention on expanding services to existing clients rather than searching for new ones.

Nevertheless, she knows that networking is an important business development tool. She has joined several businesswomen's groups and the chamber of commerce, and it has paid off. Through her various affiliations, Donna has found new clients for her one-stop shop.

Donna offers a word of warning for women considering starting a home-based business: "I would recommend that they thoroughly research their idea and make sure there is a market for it. They must have a goal or plan. The biggest failure for people who start a new business is trying to 'wing it' without doing any homework."

Donna would like to see Editype Concepts grow into a full-fledged ad agency and is working hard to make that happen. In recent days, she has also turned her entrepreneurial sights back to where it all began—the Bucks County Tennis Club. Her parents are now close to retirement, and there is nothing they want more than to leave the business they founded 21 years ago as a legacy to their daughter. Although children are not in the forecast for Donna right now, who knows? Maybe a third generation of Agnellos will come to enjoy the many benefits of running a home-based business.

CHAPTER FIFTEEN

Service Industries

Years ago, most American jobs were related to the manufacturing industry—in other words, making things to sell. Now the Asians make everything! But not to fear, Americans have discovered the value of doing things. Today, service-based industries constitute a substantial portion of the United States' economy.

A service is anything you can do for others because they are unwilling or unable to do it for themselves. It can be taking care of their dog while they're on vacation, watching their children while they're at work, or cleaning their bathroom while they watch TV. The bottom line is this: Are you willing to do it, and are people willing to pay you? If the answer to both questions is yes, you've got a viable business venture on your hands.

A major advantage of starting a service business

is that most require lots of "sweat equity" but a minimal amount of financial risk. That's because, in most instances, you are the only equipment you need. Of course, you may have to obtain special training or certification, and you might need to purchase some tools of the trade. But generally speaking, service industries require little up-front investment.

If you would like to start a home-based service, the best approach is to ask people what types of things they don't have the time or inclination to do—but must be done. Or simply make a list of the things you wish someone else would do for you: cook, clean, chauffeur your children, go to the grocery store.

Next, target your marketing to people who can afford to hire someone else to do such tasks on their behalf. For the most part, service industries are geared to middle- and upper-class prospects. Be particularly alert to people who are busy or image-conscious. That means business executives and professionals should be foremost in your mind when conjuring up service possibilities.

To give you an illustration, recall that we listed cooking on the roster of time-consuming but necessary activities. You might name your business the "Home-delivered Gourmet" or something similar. Print up flyers offering excellent meals prepared and delivered, and distribute it in upscale new developments likely to house two-income families. Mention that they can have the speed and convenience of pizza delivery or frozen dinners but with the nutrition and taste of home-cooked meals. Locate 10 families interested in your service one night per week, charge them the price of two pizzas (fifteen to twenty dollars) and you can easily earn $200 extra per week. Best of all, your only up-front investment will be the cost of printing the flyers and buying additional groceries.

When it comes to service industries, no idea is too outlandish. I recently heard of a woman who is a professional "stander in line"—that's right, she stands in lines for a very handsome hourly rate. If someone can make money standing in line, I bet your idea will fly, too.

Jinny Grisolia: Service with a Smile

In July 1986, Jinny Grisolia said good-bye to 13 years of government work to start her own day-care center. The general consensus among her coworkers was that her business venture would never succeed. But all the skepticism in the world can't stop a woman with a dream!

Jinny realized she and her husband, Frank, who was supporting three children from a previous marriage, would never be able to afford a home unless she went into business for herself. She insists she never had a doubt about her endeavor, thanks in large part to the support and encouragement of her husband. She believed it would work, and if it didn't, then she would try something else.

At the time, she was living on the third floor of an apartment building owned by her aunt. Aware of the tremendous need for quality child care, Jinny persuaded her aunt to convert the first two floors of the building into a school. The two have been 50-50 partners in Precious Moments Preschool and Day-Care Center ever since.

However, the road to Precious Moments was rocky, to say the least. When Jinny asked the local zoning commission to allow her to operate in a residential area, they turned her down. After six months in court, she finally received the go-ahead to start the center. But, needless to say, the local authorities were less than enthusiastic in assisting someone who had taken them to court—and won.

Aside from the zoning difficulties, Jinny was amazed at how many state and federal requirements had to be met: special fire walls, a sprinkler system, bathroom facilities, and on and on. All of this, of course, cost money. But when Jinny went to the bank to apply for a $30,000 business loan, they told her to forget it! By her own admission, Jinny had absolutely no collateral of any kind. Fortunately, her aunt was willing to put up her house as collateral, and they eventually managed to get loans totaling $24,000 from two separate banks.

Unfortunately, they spent every penny of it on renovations before they even opened. As a result, the first year was very difficult financially. In fact, Jinny not only didn't receive a salary, she was

$800 short of meeting her business expenses each month. Thanks to the volunteer work of many family members, they managed to make it through.

Eight kids showed up on opening day in September 1986. Since that time, the school has mushroomed, peaking at an enrollment of 90 students in 1988. Jinny now has four full-time and five part-time employees. The dramatic growth of the school is a credit to Jinny's determination to make Precious Moments a warm and loving environment.

One of the most gratifying moments for Jinny was the day she and her husband purchased the home that once seemed an impossible dream. "Even though Frank doesn't really express it, I know he's relieved he doesn't have to worry about how we're going to make ends meet," Jinny says. "I've been able to take some of the stress and responsibility off his shoulders, and that feels great."

Jinny can identify with the challenge of balancing home and business, even though her three stepchildren come only for the weekends. In the beginning, she worked 12 hours per day, five days a week. "I look back on it now and say, 'How did I do it?' But I did. I managed to get everything done, but don't ask me how. Now I work only three days a week."

According to Jinny, operating a service-oriented business has provided unexpected rewards. Her

day-care center has brought Jinny into contact with
children and families whom she otherwise would
never have been able to influence. "Close to 50 percent of the children in our school come from single-
parent families, and we have quite a few who live
with Dad, only because Mom doesn't want the
responsibility," she says. "Whenever I talk to parents about their kids, whether it's good or bad, I try
to show them kindness and gentleness. I try to be a
reflection of Jesus in the way I act. It feels good to
know I can influence the children who come to our
center. In that way, this business is also a ministry."

CHAPTER SIXTEEN

Direct Sales

Direct sales is a $25 billion industry employing an estimated 9.3 million Americans, 60 percent of whom are women. Sales is a field in which women have consistently excelled. Why? Because success in sales is a result of hard work and building relationships—two things at which women are particularly good.

Direct sales also allows you to set your own hours and career pace and, in many cases, be your own boss. Often, work can be done in the evening, when your husband or friends are available to watch the children. If delivering products is part of your job, no one will mind if you bring the children along.

Two major avenues of direct sales exist: person-to-person and party plan, which involves having a group of people gather at someone's home.

Your personality determines which is right for you. Some people are too intimidated to speak in front of a group and would rather relate to people individually. Others find the party plan less stressful emotionally, because if one person isn't interested in your products, others in the group will help soften the blow.

The key to successful direct sales is choosing a company and product line you believe in and feel good about representing. Ask yourself these questions:

1. Does the company have a good reputation?
2. Do they offer employee benefits?
3. Are there advancement opportunities?
4. Is an up-front investment required?
5. Do you have to purchase a starter kit?
6. Will they provide training?
7. Are the products high quality?
8. Is it a legitimate business or an illegal pyramid scheme?

You should also consider how the products are delivered. In some instances, you have to deliver the products personally (Avon); other companies ship directly to the customer (Discovery Toys). One method is not necessarily better than another; there are advantages and disadvantages to each. Company delivery is more convenient for you, while personal delivery offers more sales opportunities. Again, it depends on your preference.

There are an estimated 300 to 400 direct sales companies operating in the United States today, offering everything from toys and clothing to cleaning and health care products. Some are more reputable than others. If you are seriously considering joining an organization and have questions about credibility, contact the Direct Selling Association, 1730 M Street NW, Suite 610, Washington, D.C. 20036, or check out their Web site: www.dsa.org.

Be particularly wary of companies that require a large investment or promise quick wealth. In this arena, the old adage is as true as ever: If it sounds too good to be true, it is. Also, watch out for any sales organization that stresses recruiting new members, rather than selling products. Such tactics often constitute an illegal pyramid scheme.

Olga Power: Filling Her Empty Nest with Merchandise

Put away that rocking chair. This 62-year-old grandmother of 16 is definitely not interested in sitting around. She conducts a busy and successful sales operation. But at first, it looked like finding her niche might be tough.

Olga Power dropped out of school after the ninth grade and took a job at a five-and-dime store. Not long afterward, she married and began raising a family. She recalls those days: "When you're raising eight kids, you're so busy all the time that you don't even realize how busy you are. Until it stops." Today, all of her children are grown. She describes the empty-nest syndrome as a "traumatic" experience. "I poured my life into those children for years, and when they were gone I went through a time when I didn't know what to do with myself." She decided to fill her days with work.

Initially, Olga felt her career options were very limited, because she lacked formal education. She tried cashiering jobs—after 40-plus years of mothering, she knew she could count change. But the pay was low and the working conditions were even worse. She then tried turning her love of crafts into a business venture and was moderately successful. However, it wasn't until she found a job as a home demonstrator with House of Lloyd that she began to blossom.

One of the things Olga likes best about her work is meeting new people, and she meets all types. She says, "I've been in the homes of very wealthy people, and I've been in homes where they could barely afford to buy a bottle of soda for refreshments. It's been a fascinating experience." Mostly, she likes keeping busy. "I'm not just sitting home getting older and older," she says. "I'm keeping my mind active."

The fact that she can simultaneously Christmas shop is an added bonus. Once her selling season is over, she's free to do whatever she wants with the merchandise in her sales kit. These days, birthdays and anniversaries are all taken care of with last year's product line. Her children and grandchildren don't seem to mind!

She finds the party plan well-suited to her, because it's less threatening than one-on-one sales. There's always at least one person at every party who is genuinely interested in the merchandise, and she'll focus her sales effort there.

Finding customers has not been as much of a problem as she had initially anticipated. The first thing she did was call her children. Each of her four daughters booked a house party, and from there the parties just seemed to multiply.

Olga obviously enjoys what she does and feels she has the best of both worlds: the security of an employer and the independence of working for herself. The company unconditionally guarantees everything she sells, and she doesn't have to hassle with collecting money or making product deliveries.

She also likes working only when she wants to. But that doesn't mean she sits back and takes it easy. She consistently finishes in first place in her sales district. What keeps her motivated? A dream vacation to Hawaii. The company offers a free trip to employees who achieve a certain sales level each year.

Olga attributes her success to a combination of "ambition and bullheadedness." She knew a lot of people thought she'd never make it, and that motivated her to keep going. Still, there are times when the last thing she wants to do is load up the car and travel to a stranger's house to sell merchandise. "But I get up and go anyway," she says.

"Afterward, I feel better about myself."

Although her family has been supportive, she takes her share of good-natured kidding. "I get a lot of teasing from my kids. I've been called Mrs. Lloyd by more than one person in my family." Her husband, Jack, also worries that she's too old to work. But she insists: "I'm not going to let myself be an old lady. I'm going to keep working as long as God gives me strength."

What About MLMs (Multilevel Marketing Companies)?

No doubt about it, the divide-and-multiply approach used by MLMs is a great marketing strategy. I personally know several people (including Rhonda Anderson, co-founder of Creative Memories, and Mariette Holland, founder of Mariette Internationale) who have grown their businesses exponentially by recruiting others to sell their products. Their purpose in creating an MLM was to build an affordable and effective product distribution system. Distributors receive a commission on sales, plus residual income by recruiting still others to market the products.

Here's the difference between a legitimate MLM and an illegal pyramid scheme: Legit companies emphasize selling products and recruiting others to sell them; pyramids emphasize recruiting for recruiting's sake. It is *against the law* to run a business whose sole purpose is to recruit others who in turn recruit others, and on and on. Of course, all MLMs offer products, but if it's a fraudulent company, the products are only incidental.

Before signing up, ask yourself:

1. Where is the company's emphasis—on their great products or on how easy it will be to make money by calling people you went to grade-school with?
2. Are the products unique and reasonably priced?
3. Does the company offer training in the use and sale of the products?
4. How much up-front investment is required? It shouldn't cost more than a few hundred dollars.
5. Are you required to sell a certain amount each month in order to maintain your position? This is how people end up with a garage full of unsold products.
6. Do you have a knack for selling? Don't let anyone tell you the products sell themselves. That's another way to end up with a garage full of inventory.

Yes, you can successfully work at home through an MLM company—just make sure you don't get roped into an illegal pyramid scheme instead.

CHAPTER SEVENTEEN

Business Support Services

Home-based business support services are springing up all over the place these days—and for good reason. First, because many women have secretarial and other office support experience. Second, affordable computer systems make it easy to transfer skills obtained in the work place to a home-based business. And there is a great demand for it.

According to Lynette Smith, executive director of the Association of Business Support Services International, approximately 20,000 Americans now offer some type of office support service. She suggests that the average home-based businesswoman, working full time, can hope to gross $25,0000 to $35,000 per year. The minimal initial investment ranges from $3,000 to $5,000 on up. "You can do it cheaper," notes Smith, "but it will take much longer and you'll have to really pound the pavement."

Many students, professors, job hunters, sales representatives, doctors, lawyers, and insurance agents have need of office support but not a full-time secretary. Offices with work overflow may also use business support services. If you possess secretarial skills and are interested in starting a home-based service, there are a number of excellent books that will show you exactly how to get started. Visit your local library or www.amazon.com for a current list of books available.

While it's possible to make good money doing this kind of work, there are disadvantages as well. You must be willing to work evenings and weekends, and many of your customers will need their work done yesterday. The nature of the business will require a lot of direct contact with the public, so you'll be expected to dress professionally.

The up-front investment can vary greatly, depending upon the equipment you purchase. Wendy Brooks (featured later in this chapter) spent $500 to launch her typing service with a used typewriter, but that was almost 20 years ago. To start such a business today, you'll probably have to invest thousands of dollars to purchase state-of-the-art equipment and several thousand more to promote your business through the phone book, direct mail, and networking.

In today's competitive market, a computer, laser printer, and desktop publishing software are mandatory. In addition, you may eventually want to purchase transcription, fax, and photocopy machines.

Unless you have a solid secretarial background, a career in word processing is probably not right for you. You will need to be familiar with various letter formats, type styles, and general office procedures. For maximum efficiency, it is also vital to know your software package extremely well.

If you're interested in a secretarial business, there are two very helpful organizations worth checking out:

Association of Business Support Services
   International
22875 Savi Ranch Parkway
Suite H
Yorba Linda, CA 92887
1-800-237-1462
www.abssi.org

This educational association offers a start-up manual called "Starting a Successful Office Support Service" ($20), a monthly magazine, toll-free consultation line, and annual conventions.

American Association of Medical
   Transcriptionists
P.O. Box 576187
Modesto, CA 95357-6187
1-800-982-2182
www.aamt.org

This association offers a bimonthly trade journal, catalog, and library resource, an annual convention, plus information on starting a transcription business.

Wendy Brooks: Moving Beyond Home

For 15 years, Wendy Brooks was someone's secretary. Today, she's the boss. She is the founder of Brooks Office Services, which provides typing, photocopying, and fax transmission services for local businesspeople, students, and anyone else who happens to stop in her storefront business. The company also provides permanent and temporary job-placement services, as well as word processing classes.

Wendy had been enduring a long commute for four years and was fed up with the pressure and wasted time. Realizing all those traffic hours could be utilized more productively, she decided to convert her recreation room into an office and go into business for herself. With a $500 loan from her mother, she bought a used desk and typewriter, wrote a detailed business plan and was open for business within two weeks.

Wendy's equipment may have been second-hand, but her service was first-class from the beginning. She realized that if she wanted to be considered a professional, she had to look professional. As a result, she woke up every morning at seven and got dressed (right down to stockings and pumps), just as she would have if she were still working in an office. She recalls, "Some of the people who used my service were businessmen, and a lot of them came to my door in business suits. They didn't want to be greeted by someone in shorts or sweats."

Wendy was equally serious about her business conduct. She reported for work in her home office every day, rain or shine, just as she would have if she weren't the boss. Some people, especially some family members, thought this type of self-discipline was a bit excessive. But there can be no doubt that her efforts have paid off. In fact, she credits her success in large measure to that self-discipline and determination.

Wendy feels her business success has affected the way her family views her. Even though her kids are older now, she senses that her business has been an inspiration to them. Her husband's initial reaction was to let her get it out of her system. Now he takes it seriously. "I've heard him refer to it as our business," she says. "I even once heard him say 'my' business, and I said, 'Wait a minute! I can live with the *our* business, but I can't live with the *your* business!'"

Wendy feels her career has strengthened her marriage because there's more emphasis on teamwork now. Her husband has become involved with her business and helps out around the house. "Whoever gets home first cooks," Wendy says. "Whoever has strength after the meal does the dishes. Nobody's keeping score."

As for her household, she says it's as organized as it needs to be. "I used to spend too much time worrying about nit-picky little things," she says. "It was just because I had nothing better to do. When you devote time to your business, some other things, like housework, have to be let go. And guess what? The sun still rises the next day, and no one gets any incurable diseases."

Wendy never intended to become an overnight sensation, preferring instead to build her company gradually, making sure the foundations were secure. Nevertheless, growth has come at an average of 50 percent per year.

The hardest step for Wendy was moving the business out of her home. When her operation grew to the point that she had an average of six to 10 people coming to her house every day, some of them late at night, she knew something had to give. Although the neighbors didn't say anything about the disruption to their quiet residential street, she knew it wasn't fair to them.

The heavy volume of traffic through the house (there was no separate business entrance) was also taking its toll on her family life. Wendy realized she had two options: deliberately scale back the business by eliminating clients or move to an office.

She decided to go full speed ahead, but the decision didn't come easily. When the business was in the privacy of her own home, it was much less intimidating. If it didn't work out, she could always quit. But opening up shop on Main Street was a different story altogether. "The scariest thing was hanging up the sign 'Coming Soon' because I was saying to the world, 'I'm here. I'm taking a chance.'"

Taking that chance has paid off. Today, Brooks Office Services has over one hundred clients serviced by a staff of six. Wendy's placement service is doing very well. For the temporary secretarial service, she maintains a pool of 10 to 15 secretaries, in addition to finding permanent jobs for about two dozen secretaries a year. Now Wendy is considering opening a school to train legal and medical secretaries.

The business is not the only thing growing. Wendy is growing personally, as well. This fall, she'll be attending college for the first time. She plans to study business management and marketing. But Wendy is surprisingly modest about her success. "I really don't believe I have any more going for me than anyone else does," she says. "I think if anything I just have stick-to-itiveness."

She also has a philosophy emblazoned on her office wall: "Whatever you vividly imagine, ardently desire, sincerely believe, and enthusiastically act upon, must inevitably come to pass." That's a powerful recipe for success.

CHAPTER EIGHTEEN

A New Era for Women Entrepreneurs

Women entrepreneurs are one of the fastest-growing segments of American business today. The array of opportunities available is as diverse as the women themselves. But one thing is certain—women in massive numbers are moving into the ranks of entrepreneurs. According to the United States Small Business Administration, by the year 2000 approximately 50 percent of all self-employed entrepreneurs will be women.

What is an entrepreneur? Someone with a vision for a new product or service, and the courage to make it a reality. Opportunities abound for those who are creative enough to offer solutions to the problems faced by Americans today. In our fast-paced society, people are crying out for assistance in managing the many facets of their complex lives. They want personal and professional services:

child care, health care, home care, yard care, car
care—every kind of care! If you can provide a
needed service, there's a place for you in today's
market.

Of course, no one loves gadgets more than
Americans. If you can come up with a product to
help people organize their closets, entertain their
children or spruce up their yard, there's bound to
be someone willing to buy it.

If you have fashioned a device to solve a
household problem, turn it into a product.
Chances are, other people are faced with the same
problem and would be willing to pay money to
obtain your time-saving, aggravation-saving, or
space-saving solution.

Truly, the possibilities are only as limited as
your imagination. Chapter 19 lists hundreds of
ideas for a home-based business, and no doubt
another 200 suggestions could have been included.
All you need to do is pick an idea and run with it.

Rhonda Anderson: Building on Passion

There's no better way to build a business than
with passion. If you believe strongly enough that
people need your product, you're bound to succeed. Rhonda Anderson is living proof.

In 1985, finances were tight for Rhonda and
her family. Her husband, Mac, worked as a car-
penter. Sometimes the hours were long and tiring;
other times there was no work at all. To make
matters worse, the Andersons could not get health

insurance—a serious concern for a family raising four children in cold Montana winters.

Rhonda knew she needed to do something, yet she knew her children needed her at home. First, she tried baby-sitting. Unfortunately, repairing the damage caused to her house and furniture by the kids she watched actually cost more than she earned. Next she tried tole-painting children's furniture, but it was time-consuming and generated very little profit.

Not willing to give up on working at home, Rhonda and her husband purchased five acres of land to subdivide. Rhonda handled all aspects of dividing and selling the lots. In addition to selling the land, the Andersons built some of the homes. That arrangement worked well until the real estate market crashed in 1984.

It wasn't until January 1987 that Rhonda finally found her niche. One afternoon, Rhonda's sister called her in a panic. The woman coordinating crafts for the MOPS (Mothers of Preschoolers) program had to cancel.

Rhonda agreed to spend an hour showing the ladies how to organize an attractive scrapbook photo album, combining pictures, mementos, report cards, crafts, and so on. Rhonda felt strongly about the importance of building family togetherness through scrapbooks. She wanted to convey how much it encouraged and strengthened her family.

Rhonda spent the next three days preparing.

She analyzed how she put together her scrapbooks and why they were better than regular photo albums. She prepared a handout, explaining that family scrapbooks are important because they build self-esteem and preserve family history.

The response from the MOPS group was overwhelming. After the meeting, the women flooded Rhonda with questions. They also placed orders for 40 scrapbook photo albums. (The albums were not available in stores, so Rhonda agreed to coordinate the order.) Rhonda recalls, "I thought everyone preserved their family photos as carefully as I did. My mother always made scrapbooks, and I just naturally continued the tradition. To me, it wasn't a big deal."

But to others it was a big deal. Soon Rhonda's neighbors wanted to host scrapbook parties. Rhonda realized that most people collect photographs for years, without ever organizing them. And few people know that most photo albums contain chemicals that gradually destroy photographs.

Rhonda knew she was on to a home-based business with real potential. She began to invest time and money in her new venture, called Shoebox to Showcase.

Rhonda called every church and civic group in the area, offering to present her idea. Not every group agreed to host a gathering, but many did. Over the next few months, Rhonda explained the joys of scrapbook photo albums to hundreds of people.

Her efforts quickly resulted in numerous scrapbook orders. Then an event occurred that changed the course of Rhonda's business. She received a notice from the manufacturer that supplied her with photo albums saying it was dropping the line of albums. Rhonda immediately called the company, fearing they wouldn't deliver her scrapbooks.

Cheryl Lightle, vice president of Webway, Inc., answered Rhonda's call. When Rhonda described Shoebox to Showcase, Cheryl found the concept intriguing. Eventually, Webway invited Rhonda to present her business idea to the company.

In March 1987, Rhonda met with Webway executives. Although not ready to make a commitment, the company was impressed with her idea. Encouraged by the response, she ordered business cards and bought new professional-looking clothes. She bought a van to haul her inventory and painted "Shoebox to Showcase" on the side. Then she bought a computer to keep track of everything. In all, Rhonda invested $15,000, money originally intended for a down payment on a house. Rhonda quickly ordered 1,000 more albums and sold them within four months.

That really got Webway's attention. In June 1987, they invited Rhonda to meet with them again. This time Rhonda had solid statistics to back her convictions. Thanks to her computer, she had kept meticulous records, proving the success of her sales approach.

After five days of meetings, Rhonda signed an agreement with Webway, in which they would provide her with products and marketing material. Rhonda agreed to work as a consultant, paid hourly, to promote Shoebox to Showcase nation-wide.

Rhonda recommended that the business continue using informal workshops. She believed organizing a scrapbook should be fun, not a chore. She also noticed that the workshop format improved sales.

There was just one problem. Rhonda could be only in one place at a time, yet the demand for the workshops continued to grow. In 1988, Rhonda signed on eight consultants to help her promote the business. She encouraged them to conduct their own workshops and recruit new consultants. No longer a one-woman enterprise, Shoebox to Showcase became a multilevel marketing company.

The turning point for Shoebox to Showcase came when Rhonda appeared in *Focus on the Family* magazine and on the radio broadcast. "The response was excellent," Rhonda recalls. "We heard from 8,000 people. As a result, we grew from 200 to 800 consultants in just a few short months."

As of 1999, the company, now known as Creative Memories, has 40,000 consultants in the United States, Canada, United Kingdom, and Australia, with more than $140 million in annual sales worldwide.

Rhonda is both thrilled and surprised by the company's incredible success. What began as a hobby, then evolved into a small home-based enterprise, has grown into a multimillion dollar corporation. (If you'd like more information, you can call Creative Memories at 1 800 468-9335.)

Part Four

LAUNCHING YOUR BUSINESS

CHAPTER NINETEEN

Hundreds of Things You Can Do from Home

It is important to distinguish between working at home and working from home. There are few jobs that can be done completely at home, such as day-care provider or telemarketer. Keep in mind that even a mail-order specialist must make trips to the office-supply store, print shop, and post office.

On the other hand, almost any job can be based at home—that is, home serves as your base of operations. A manufacturer's representative obviously must leave her own home to call on prospective buyers. But she can certainly make phone calls, write correspondence, and complete paperwork at home, rather than at a downtown office.

It is also important to be realistic about how much money you can potentially earn, based on the business you choose. Some of the jobs listed here can only supplement your income. For example, it would be difficult to support a family of four as a manicurist. Others, such as an accountant or lawyer, represent a full-time commitment and may require years of training. The important thing is to choose the opportunity that is right for you, based on your goals, needs, training, and interests.

Following is a list of possibilities you may want to consider for your home-based business. Read through the list quickly and mark anything that grabs your attention. Then go through a second time with a more critical eye and begin to narrow down the list to about five choices. Rank them in order of preference and begin to explore each one in turn. That means going to the library to do research, evaluating the market in your area, and weighing the various factors discussed in chapter 6 (under the subheading "What Business Is Right for You?").

Remember, the best approach is to try one option after another until you find the right one (do give each your best shot). Don't give up if you discover that a zoning regulation or some other obstacle prevents your first choice from materializing. If at first you don't succeed, try, try something else!

- Accountant
- Acting Instructor
- Advertising Agency
- Aerobics Instructor
- Animal Breeder
- Animal Boarding
- Animal Trainer
- Answering Service

- Antique Repair
- Antique Sales
- Apartment Finder
- Appliance Repair
- Aquarium Design
- Aquarium Installation
- Arts and Crafts Fair Promotion
- Art Rental
- Attorney Referral Service
- Auto Repair
- Baby Gift Basket Preparation
- Baby Bracelets and Accessories
- Baby Shoe Preserving
- Baking (for local restaurants or direct sales)
- Balloon Delivery Service
- Basket Weaving
- Beauty Salon
- Bed and Breakfast Proprietor
- Beekeeper
- Bicycle Sales and Repair
- Billing (prepare and mail invoices for other businesses)
- Birth Announcements (ceramic, pillows, etc.)
- Boarding House
- Bookbinding
- Bookkeeping
- Bridal Consultant and Wedding Planner
- Bridal Registry Service
- Business Appraiser
- Business Consultant
- Calligraphy (invitations, poems, Scripture verses)
- Cake Decorator
- Cake Decorating Instructor
- Camp and Nursery School Referral Service
- Canner
- Career Counselor
- Cartoon and Caricature Illustrator (from photographs or at events)
- Catering
- Ceramics (instructions, sales)
- Chair Caning
- Childbirth Educator
- Child Care Service
- Children's Birthday Parties
- Children's Book Writer or Illustrator

- Clipping Service (cutting out newspaper and magazine articles for specific companies)
- Closet Organizing Service
- Clowning
- Coin Dealing
- Collating and Stapling Service
- College Financial Aid Consultant
- Color Analysis
- Commercial Artist
- Communications Consultant
- Computer Consultant
- Computer Instructor
- Computer Programmer
- Consignment Shop
- Consultant (in your field of expertise)
- Cooking Instructor
- Cookbook Writer
- Copywriter
- Costume Design and Sales
- CPR Instructor
- Craft Supply Sales
- Crafts Instructor
- Crafts Sales
- Credit and Debt Counselor
- Credit Report Service
- Curtain Making
- Dance Instructor
- Data Entry
- Data Processing Service
- Day-care or Baby-sitting Service
- Decoy Design and Sales
- Delivery Service
- Desktop Publishing
- Diaper Service
- Dictation Service
- Dog Walking
- Doll (house, furniture, clothes) Design and Sales
- Doll Making
- Dressmaking and Alterations
- Driving Instructor
- Ear Piercing
- Earring Design and Sales
- Economic Advisor
- Editor
- Educational Consultant
- Electrician
- Employment Agency
- Escort Service for Children or Elderly
- Estate Appraiser and Liquidator

- Estate Planning
- Executive Search Firm
- Exercise Instructor
- Family Counselor
- Fashion Designer
- Financial Planning Consultant
- Flea Market Vendor
- Florist
- Flower Arranger
- Free-lance Writer
- Free-lance Artist
- Free-lance Commercial Artist
- Fruit Basket Preparation
- Fundraiser (for nonprofit organizations, corporations, etc.)
- Furniture Restoration
- Garage Sale Planner and Promoter
- Gardener
- Gift Basket Preparation
- Gift Buying and Wrapping
- Graphic Designer
- Greeting Card Writer
- Gymnastics Instructor
- Handbill Distribution
- Handpainted Clothing Maker
- Home Demonstrator
- Hairstyling
- Health and Fitness Consultant
- Home-Management Consultant
- Handwriting Analyst
- Handyperson
- Housekeeping Service
- House Painter (interior or exterior)
- How-To Book Writer
- Image Consultant
- Immigration and Naturalization Consultant
- Income Tax Preparation
- Information Brokerage
- Insurance Agent
- Interior Decorator
- Internet Marketing
- Internet Research
- Investment Counselor
- Janitorial Service
- Jewelry Design
- Jewelry Repair
- Jewelry Sales
- Kitchen and Bathroom Planning
- Labor Relations
- Landscape Design
- Laundering and Ironing

- Lawn and Shrub Maintenance
- Locksmith
- Magician
- Mailing List Service
- Mail-Order Business
- Management Consultant
- Manicurist
- Marketing Consultant
- Market Researcher
- Marriage Counselor
- Medical Transcription
- Messenger Service
- Monogramming
- Musical Instrument Instructor
- Nanny Agency and Referral Service
- Needlework Design
- Needlework Framing
- Newsletter Publisher
- Newspaper Delivery
- Notereader-Scopist (for court)
- Nursing (visiting nurse)
- Office Services (photocopying, fax transmission)
- Painter
- Paralegal
- Party Planner
- Payroll Preparation Service

- Pet Sitting
- Pet Transporting (to vet, airport, training school)
- Photographer (free-lance, weddings, babies, etc.)
- Photo Restoration
- Picture Framing
- Pillow Maker
- Plant Sales or Rental
- Play Group Organizer
- Pollster
- Portrait Painter
- Project Finisher (needlework, crafts)
- Proofreader
- Telecommuter
- Psychologist
- Public Opinion Analyst
- Public Relations Agency
- Public Speaking Coach
- Puppeteer
- Quilt Making
- Real Estate Appraiser
- Real Estate Sales
- Toy Making
- Researcher (for writers, attorneys, media, professors)
- Residential Manager
- Résumé Service
- Retirement Planning Service

- Reunion Planner
- Roommate Matching Service
- Rubber Stamp Making
- Salesperson (Avon, Mary Kay, Amway)
- Self-Defense Trainer
- Seminar Lecturer
- Sewing Instructor
- Shopping Service (for shut-ins, elderly, etc.)
- Singing Telegrams
- Software Designer
- Software Manual Writer or Illustrator
- Speech Therapist
- Speech Writing
- Stenciling Service
- Stencil Design and Sales
- Stockbroker
- Tailor
- Talent Agent
- Tax Planning Consultant
- Telemarketing Specialist
- Telephone Book Delivery
- Ticket Agent
- Time-Management Consultant
- Tour Guide
- Tourist Host
- Toy Selling
- Transcription
- Translator or Interpreter
- Travel Agent
- Trip Organizer
- Tutor
- Typesetter
- Typing Service
- Upholstery Repair
- Used Book Selling
- Vegetable Growing and Selling
- Video Recording
- Video Recording Instructor
- Videotape Editor
- Voice Instructor
- Wake-Up Call Service
- Wallpapering
- Wedding Coordinator-Consultant
- Wood Carving
- Word Processing Service
- Writing Service (advertising copy, brochures, flyers, articles, fillers, greeting cards)
- Web Page Designer

YOUR MOST IMPORTANT CUSTOMER

Everyone has a hero—or at least they should! Mine is Dr. Michael LeBoeuf, author of numerous books, including *How to Win Customers and Keep Them for Life.* His book *Working Smart* absolutely transformed my life when I read it back in 1982. Since his recent move to Arizona, I've been privileged to get to know him and call him a friend.

I suppose the most important thing Dr. LeBoeuf taught me is this: The most important customer you will ever win is . . . yourself. That's because enthusiasm is an emotion, and emotions are absolutely contagious. Think about it: When people start hooting and hollering for the home team, normally low-key people join in with abandon. When someone starts laughing uncontrollably, few people in the room can resist joining in. When someone cries from the heart, those around them are often moved to tears.

Here's how Dr. LeBoeuf puts it:

> There is absolutely no substitute for an honest, unshakable, enthusiastic belief that the products and services you offer are the best available anywhere. Couple that with a sincere passion for helping people and you have an unbeatable combination for creating and keeping customers. People are persuaded more by attitude than logic for two basic reasons that you should always keep in mind as you deal

with customers or with people in general:
- People are ruled by their emotions
- Emotions are contagious

In the final analysis, persuasion [winning customers] isn't converting people to your way of thinking. It's converting people to your way of feeling and believing.[1]

As I always say (with far less sophistication): BELIEVE IN YOU AND OTHERS WILL, TOO. Keep that thought foremost in your mind as you set out to launch your own business.

CHAPTER TWENTY

Business and Home Management Forms

O n the following pages are forms and charts you may photocopy or adapt for use in your home and business management. Feel free to pick and choose which of these suit your business, and tailor them to fit your need. Then, photocopy them, using the enlarge feature to produce forms customized to fit into your daily planner. Below is a list of the forms included in this chapter and some suggestions for getting the most out of them.

• Checklist for Getting Started. Double check this list of things to do to get your business rolling.

• Business Resources. Use these forms to keep track of the people who can make your business more successful—suppliers, freelancers, experts, etc.

• Children's Chore Chart. You know your children best. Customize and put this to work for you.

• Customer Contact Log. This vital form is to keep track of your conversations with your customers: what you promise to do for them, by what date and at what price. Using it faithfully will ensure that your customers stay customers.

• Conversation Log. This will serve as the second page for both your Business Resources forms and your Customer Contact Log. Using this will preclude filling in redundant information requested on the first page.

• Daily Planner. This form should be used each day to maximize your effectiveness. Before photocopying, fill in those items in your schedule that remain constant. That way, you won't need to write them over and over again each day.

• Expense Log. Since you don't want to pay more taxes than you owe, be sure to carry this form with you and use it constantly. You can maintain one central expense log or keep a separate sheet for each client if you bill back at the end of each month. I recommend you transfer your expense information regularly into your journal or computer program. Do not allow 12 months of vital information to accumulate in your notebook.

• Grocery List. Before photocopying this form, fill in products you frequently buy. Listing needed items throughout the week will help avoid extra trips to the store for forgotten groceries and supplies.

• Mileage Log. Every time you drive on a

business-related matter, be sure to note your mileage in your log. This will come in handy at tax time.

• Prospect Tracking Log. The next best thing to customers are prospects. Keep track of who you talk to, what transpires, and most importantly, when and how you should follow up.

• Projects Worksheet. This form will help you keep track of any special projects you may be working on.

• Quiet Time Worksheet. Using this form will help you organize your Bible studies and glean truths from God's Word to apply to your life.

• Things To Do Today. The busier you get, the more you'll understand the importance of this vital form.

• Time Inventory Chart. This is the key to your all-important time tracking exercise. List up to 30 activities you frequently do, such as bathing and dressing the children, packing lunches, etc. I've included 10 common activities to get you started. Once your numbering system is worked out, you can simply write the appropriate number in the corresponding time slot. (It's easier to plug in numbers than write out the activities each time.)

• Weekly Evaluation. This form is especially helpful as you're starting up your business. It will serve as a guidepost for tracking progress. As you become busier and more efficient, you may find it less necessary.

Checklist for Getting Started

Date Completed   Task

_____   Complete Skills and Interests
            Inventory to determine what business
            is right for you (page 81)

_____   Complete goal setting exercise (page
            31). Check state, county, and city zon-
            ing code restrictions. Obtain necessary
            permits and licenses for operation.
            Check deed or lease for any restrictions

_____   Discuss with neighbors if your busi-
            ness will involve any additional traf-
            fic, parking, noise, etc.

_____   Determine legal structure:
            ❏ Sole Proprietorship
            ❏ Partnership
            ❏ Corporation

_____   Complete necessary paperwork (trade
            name certificate, partnership agree-
            ment or articles of incorporation, etc.)

_____   Develop a business plan (page 86)

_____   Develop a marketing plan

_____   Develop start-up and first-year operat-
            ing budgets (pages 184-186)

_____   Set up your home office. Set up a fil-
            ing system. Set up a record-keeping
            system. Open a business checking
            account. Apply for a loan, if warranted

_____ Meet with your insurance agent to determine if additional insurance is required

_____ If you will be hiring employees, apply for an employer identification number

_____ Register trademarks and logos. Obtain business cards and stationery. Develop and print a brochure. Begin advertising. Write and distribute a press release

Business Resources

Category: _____

Company Name: _____
Address: _____
_____
Contact Name: _____
Title: _____
Phone #: _____ Fax #: _____

Description of Products/Services Offered: _____
_____
_____
_____
_____

Conversation Log

Date	Key Discussion Points	Date for Follow-up

Children's Chore Chart Week

Week _____

Chore	Whose Job	Sun	Mon	Tues	Wed	Thurs	Fri	Sat

Customer Contact Log

Company Name: _____

Address: _____

_____

Contact Name: _____

Title: _____

Contact Name: _____

Title: _____

Personal Info: _____

_____

Phone #: _____ Fax #: _____

Customer History

Date Met: _____ Where: _____

How Introduced: _____

Conversation Log

Date	Key Discussion Points	Date for Follow-up

Daily Planner

Customer: _____   Page # _____

Time	Project	Completed
6:00 A		
7:00 A		
8:00 A		
9:00 A		
10:00 A		
11:00 A		
12:00 P		
1:00 P		
2:00 P		
3:00 P		
4:00 P		
5:00 P		
6:00 P		
7:00 P		
8:00 P		
9:00 P		
10:00 P		
11:00 P		

Today's #1 Goal: _____

Expense Log

Client: _____

Date	Description	Amount
	TOTAL	

Grocery List

Beverages	Bread
Rice/Noodles	Milk
Canned Food	Butter
Condiments:	Eggs
_____	Juice
_____	Dairy Products:
_____	_____
_____	_____
Toothpaste	Hamburger
Deodorant	Chicken
Shampoo/Conditioner	Roast
Hairspray/Styling Gel	Other Meat:
Bath Soap/Face Soap	_____
Other Grooming Products:	_____
_____	_____
_____	_____
Dish Detergent	Cheese
Laundry Detergent	Lunchmeats:
Glass Cleaner	_____
_____	_____
_____	_____
Furniture Polish	_____
Other Cleaners:	_____
_____	Frozen Food:
_____	_____
Paper Towels	_____
Napkins	_____
Tissues	Fruits & Vegetables:
Toilet Paper	_____
Plastic Wrap	_____
Aluminum Foil	_____
Other Paper Products:	_____
_____	_____
_____	_____

This Week's Menu

	Breakfast	Lunch	Dinner
Sun.			
Mon.			
Tues.			
Wed.			
Thurs.			
Fri.			
Sat.			

Mileage Log

Date	Destination	Purpose	Start/ End	Deduction

Prospect Tracking Log

Company Name: _____

Address: _____

_____

Contact Name: _____

Title: _____

Phone #: _____ Fax #: _____

How Contacted: _____

Date: _____

Comments: _____

_____

_____

_____

_____

Follow-up Contact

Date	Outcome	Next Step

Projects Worksheet

Idea: _____
_____
_____
_____

Objective: _____
_____
_____
_____

Cons: Pros:

_____   _____
_____   _____
_____   _____
_____   _____
_____   _____
_____   _____

People to Contact for Information or Assistance:

_____   _____
_____   _____
_____   _____

Action Plan

1. _____
2. _____
3. _____
4. _____
5. _____

Quiet Time Worksheet

Date: _____   Passage: _____

1. Summarize in a few sentences what the passage is about:

2. Is there an *example* for me to *follow*?

3. Is there an *error* I need to *avoid*?

4. Is there a *command* for me to *obey*?

5. Is there a *sin* I need to *forsake*?

6. What application of this passage can I make *today*?

Things To Do Today

Date: _____

	Item	Completed
Business Priorities:		
1.	_____	❏
2.	_____	❏
3.	_____	❏
4.	_____	❏
5.	_____	❏
6.	_____	❏
7.	_____	❏
8.	_____	❏
9.	_____	❏
10.	_____	❏

Family Priorities:

1.	_____	❏
2.	_____	❏
3.	_____	❏
4.	_____	❏
5.	_____	❏

Spiritual Priorities:

1.	_____	❏
2.	_____	❏
3.	_____	❏

Notes: _____

_____

Time Inventory

Week of: _____

Time	Mon	Tues	Wed	Thur	Fri	Sat	Sun	Activity
6:00								1. Spiritual
6:30								2. Reading
7:00								3. TV
7:30								4. Phone
8:00								5. Grooming
8:30								6. Meals
9:00								7. Eating
9:30								8. Dishes
10:00								9. Sleeping
10:30								10. Cleaning
11:00								11.
11:30								12.
12:00								13.
12:30								14.
1:00								15.
1:30								16.
2:00								17
2:30								18.
3:00								19.
3:30								20.
4:00								21.
4:30								22.
5:00								23.
5:30								24.
6:00								25.
6:30								26.
7:00								27.
7:30								28.
8:00								29.
8:30								30.
9:00								
9:30								
10:00								
10:30								

Adapted from Michael LeBoeuf's *Working Smart: How to Accomplish More in Half the Time*.

Weekly Evaluation Worksheet

1. What did I study in my quiet times this week?

2. Which of my business and personal goals did I pursue?

3. Which of my goals did I fail to pursue?

4. Did I attend to the important or merely urgent?

5. Am I using my unique gifts to develop my business?

6. Am I spending time in my office each day?

7. How's my business going?

8. What specific goals do I have for the coming week?

CHAPTER TWENTY-ONE

Resources Available to You

As you prepare to launch your business, you may feel anxiety about making such a big leap all by yourself. Even though you may be a sole proprietor, there are a multitude of government agencies, trade associations, and private individuals available to help you along the way. Do not hesitate to reach out for assistance to any of the resources listed here.

Again, read this portion of the book with a pen in hand. Circle or highlight any suggested resources you feel are worth pursuing. Then be sure to follow up by placing a phone call or e-mailing a request for information.

U.S. Small Business Administration (SBA)

The Small Business Administration is an independent government agency established by

Congress for the express purpose of assisting small businesses. There are over a hundred SBA offices throughout the country that provide loans, management advice, counseling, helpful brochures, and more. Be sure to contact the one nearest you. You can find them on the Internet at www.sba.gov.

Small Business Development Centers (SBDCs)

SBDCs are sponsored by the SBA in partnership with state and local governments, educational institutions, and the private sector. They are frequently affiliated with state colleges. SBDCs can provide you with counseling and training services for very modest fees (and often at no cost). There are over 500 SBDCs in 42 states. You can find more information, including a state-by-state listing of SBDC locations, at their Web site: www.smallbiz.suny.edu/

Service Corps of Retired Executives (SCORE)

SCORE consists of over 12,000 volunteer retired business executives who provide training and free management counseling to small businesses. SCORE is a great place to start since they will most likely be aware of many other resources available in your local area.

Pick up the phone and schedule an appointment with SCORE as soon as you have a business plan in mind. SCORE has an awesome Web site, jam-packed with helpful information. Check it out: www.score.org.

Small Business Institute (SBI)

The U.S. Chamber of Commerce SBIs are located on approximately 500 college campuses throughout the United States. They provide in-depth training and counseling to small business owners. Contact your area colleges to see if this service is available. Or online: http://www.us chamber.org/sbi/index.html

Small Business Answer Desk: 1 (800) 827-5722

The Answer Desk is operated by the SBA's Office of Advocacy. It is an excellent source for information concerning all aspects of running a small business. Especially helpful is the free Directory of Business Development Publications, one of which is bound to answer any question you might have. And best of all, it's free. You can call between 8:30 A.M. and 5:00 P.M. (EST), Monday through Friday. If you live in Washington, D.C., call 653-7561.

Department of Commerce, Office of Business Liaison (OBL)

OBL provides information on all business assistance programs available through federal agencies. You can obtain a complete listing by calling (202) 377-3176. Or online: http://www.osec.doc.gov/obl/

State and Local Agencies/State Economic Development Agencies

No matter which state you live in, most jobs are provided by small business owners. As a result, most states have agencies specifically designed to assist small businesses. These agencies can provide you with valuable information on the opportunities available within your state and the best types of businesses to start.

City or County Development Agencies

These exist for the same purposes as the state development agencies but are specifically concerned with their own jurisdiction.

Chambers of Commerce

Most cities, and even small towns, have a chamber of commerce that promotes local business activity. Your local chamber is an excellent source of information on business opportunities in your area and a great place to begin your networking.

Local Colleges

In addition to offering college-credit courses in a wide variety of business-related subjects such as finance, management, accounting, and economics, many colleges offer low-cost business seminars to the community.

Local Library

There is a lot of helpful information at your

local library, so take advantage of it. Libraries can be intimidating, but if you ask for assistance, most librarians are more than happy to be of service (particularly if you go during off-peak hours).

CHAPTER TWENTY-TWO

Recommended Reading List

Donna's Favorite Home Business Books

The Perfect Business by Dr. Michael LeBouef

Making It On Your Own by Paul and Sarah Edwards

Working from Home by Paul and Sarah Edwards

The Home Office and Small Business Answer Book by Janet Attard

Books on Choosing the Right Business

Work with Passion: How to Do What You Love for a Living by Nancy Anderson

Finding Your Perfect Work by Paul and Sarah Edwards

Do What You Love, the Money Will Follow by Marsha Sinetar

Books on Making the Most of Your Life

Working Smart by Dr. Michael LeBoeuf
The 7 Habits of Highly Effective People by
Stephen Covey

Books on Marketing

Getting Business to Come to You by Paul and
Sarah Edwards, with Laura Clampitt Douglas
*How to Win Customers and Keep Them for
Life* by Dr. Michael LeBoeuf
How to Promote Your Own Business by Gary
Blake and Robert W. Bly

Books About Your Particular Business

In the first edition of *Homemade Business,* I
included a list of books on starting specific businesses. However, I soon realized that the shelf life
of a book is usually very short indeed. Most books
survive for only a year or two. As a result, the
book list was frustrating for readers who spent
hours searching for out-of-print books.

Today, thanks to the Internet, there's an easier
way to find books on your proposed business. Go
to www.amazon.com, which is billed as the
world's largest bookstore, and type in the nature
of your business, whether it's accounting or pet
grooming. Within seconds, Amazon will provide
you with a list of books currently available.
Within minutes, you can place your online order.
And within days, the book will arrive at your front
door. That's a whole lot easier than traipsing off to
the library in search of nonexistent books.

Notes

Chapter 1

1. Larry Burkett estimated child care costs at $300 per month for one, $450 for two. But that didn't include all the extra visits to the doctor and pharmacy, because kids in child care are sick more often. Plus all the birthday parties, field trips, etc., that inevitably arise. I think $450 is a conservative figure.

Chapter 4

1. For more information, see Betty Beach's *Integrating Work and Family Life* (Albany, N.Y.: State University of New York Press, 1989).

Chapter 11

1. SBA publication: "Selecting the Legal Structure for Your Firm."

Chapter 12

1. Information taken verbatim from the IRS website.

Chapter 13

1. Excerpted from *The Perfect Business* by Dr. Michael LeBoeuf, p. 12-13.

Chapter 19

1. *How to Win Customers and Keep Them for Life,* by Dr. Michael LeBoeuf.

FOCUS ON THE FAMILY®
Welcome to the Family!

Whether you received this book as a gift, borrowed it from a friend, or purchased it yourself, we're glad you read it! It's just one of the many helpful, insightful, and encouraging resources produced by Focus on the Family.

In fact, that's what Focus on the Family is all about— providing inspiration, information, and biblically based advice to people in all stages of life.

It began in 1977 with the vision of one man, Dr. James Dobson, a licensed psychologist and author of 16 best-selling books on marriage, parenting, and family. Alarmed by the societal, political, and economic pressures that were threatening the existence of the American family, Dr. Dobson founded Focus on the Family with one employee—an assistant—and a once-a-week radio broadcast, aired on only 36 stations.

Now an international organization, Focus on the Family is dedicated to preserving Judeo-Christian values and strengthening the family through more than 70 different ministries, including eight separate daily radio broadcasts; television public service announcements; 11 publications; and a steady series of award-winning books, films, and videos for people of all ages and interests.

Recognizing the needs of, as well as the sacrifices and important contribution made by, such diverse groups as educators, physicians, attorneys, crisis pregnancy center staff, and single parents, Focus on the Family offers specific outreaches to uphold and minister to these individuals, too. And it's all done for one purpose, and one purpose only: to encourage and strengthen individuals and families through the life-changing message of Jesus Christ.

• • •

For more information about the ministry, or if we can be of help to your family, simply write to Focus on the Family, Colorado Springs, CO 80995 or call 1-800-A-FAMILY (1-800-232-6459). Friends in Canada may write Focus on the Family, P.O. Box 9800, Stn. Terminal, Vancouver, B.C. V6B 4G3 or call 1-800-661-9800. Visit our Web site—www.family.org—to learn more about the ministry or to find out if there is a Focus on the Family office in your country.

We'd love to hear from you!

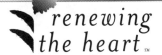